Frances William

MISOGYNY

Men who despise women

Frances William

MISOGYNY

Men who despise women

MEMOIRS

Cirencester

MEMOIRS
PUBLISHING

1A The Wool Market Dyer Street Cirencester Gloucestershire GL7 2PR
An imprint of Memoirs Publishing www.mereobooks.com

Misogyny: 978-1-86151-337-3

First published in Great Britain in 2016
by Mereo Books, an imprint of Memoirs Publishing

The address for Memoirs Publishing Group Limited can be found at
www.memoirspublishing.com

The Memoirs Publishing Group Ltd Reg. No. 7834348

The Memoirs Publishing Group supports both The Forest Stewardship Council® (FSC®) and the
PEFC® leading international forest-certification organisations. Our books carrying both the FSC
label and the PEFC® and are printed on FSC®-certified paper. FSC® is the only
forest-certification scheme supported by the leading environmental organisations including
Greenpeace. Our paper procurement policy can be found at
www.memoirspublishing.com/environment

Typeset in 11/16pt Goudy
by Wiltshire Associates Publisher Services Ltd. Printed and bound in Great Britain by
Printondemand-Worldwide, Peterborough PE2 6XD

PROLOGUE

One night Clare dreamed she was under sentence of death. She had travelled back to the 1960s, when the death penalty was still in force in England and you would be given three clear Sundays to repent before your execution. She dreamed she was in a cell which was so comfortable that you could almost call it a bedsitter. She could go out into the short corridor outside where there were rooms; they all had a few pieces of furniture, yet no one was in them. The prison officers were more like nurses, young girls who were so kind and gentle. That was all she saw. They seemed sincerely sorry that she had lost her appeal and kept giving her words of comfort by saying that right up to the last moment the Home Secretary might give her a reprieve. 'You never know what might come up,' they told her.

Then, in her dream, the day of execution came. It was nine o'clock in the morning and the prison officials marched her out to be hanged. Yet they were going in the wrong direction; they turned left instead of right. They opened a door - they were letting her out. She was faced with open spaces, garden, fields and woods. 'We'll just have to hope it gets overlooked that we didn't carry out the execution' said one of them.

But how was she going to manage? It reminded her of the wilderness at the end of her road in East Cliff, just up the steps on the white cliffs of Dover. How often she had walked amongst all that, completely bewildered, and in this dream she was back again in this world, this wide and wicked world. She knew no one; she had no support...

CHAPTER 1

It could have been the opening chapter to a horror story. Early on a dark winter's night Olive was coming in through the back way, and through the window she could see her husband James in the kitchen with a neighbour. They were making coffee, and the neighbour was helping himself to some biscuits from a cupboard. A bit of a liberty, Olive said to herself, but then people do take liberties sometimes, and she thought no more about it.

Then suddenly the man turned round. It was like a vision of Dracula. He was not the person she had thought he was but Peter, one of the most hated men in town. She knew James had invited him in because he hated her. He wanted to show her she had to accept what he said. The realisation went through her like a knife. Maybe it was the weirdness of it all that made it so difficult for her to cope with.

She turned away and went round to the front door instead. James came out of the kitchen and met her in the hall, and he was relieved to see her going straight up the stairs and not into the kitchen. He didn't know she had been in the back yard or that she knew all too well who was in there with him.

For some reason he didn't want her to know just then that he had invited Peter into their house, yet he did intend very shortly to rub her nose in it, by letting him move in as a lodger. He was going to make it clear to her that she would have to accept him. She would be forced to share the bathroom, kitchen and sitting room with him. When they were watching the television in the evening, he'd be there watching it with them.

She went upstairs several times in the next few hours. James must have heard her, yet he never came out once to see what she was doing. In fact, she was packing her things and leaving him.

It wasn't until eleven o'clock that night that Olive had everything together and was ready to leave. She knew James was in the front room downstairs. She peeped through the hole in the door where a lock had once been and saw him there, waiting for her to burst in and start a row with him. Indeed, he was good at winding her up, getting her to do things like that, for much as she wanted a quiet life, he was determined not to let her have one. Yet he seemed to be standing there as though to defend himself, as though he believed he was her helpless victim. Why? She had done so much to try to make him happy, yet he didn't want it. It was very strange.

She opened the front door and slipped down the road into the snow and out of sight. It was New Year's Eve. She went down to the bus station in Altrincham to catch the National Express coach to London; it wasn't much of a walk. She had somewhere to go in London.

A misogynist doesn't necessarily hate all women; he only hates those who come into a certain category. He cannot cope with the combination of his fear of them with his need for them. James needed his wife, yet he feared her, and fear can be so near to hate.

The bus drove slowly out of the bus station before it picked up speed along the Dunham road to start its long journey. Olive was exhausted. She began to think of all that had happened, the whole of her childhood, and then she started to doze and dream. She had been born into a loving family full of men, as well as having a very good mother. She had had an excellent father and had been surrounded by loving uncles and a very good grandfather. Some of them had been born back in the 1880s, so they belonged to a generation in which it was normal for women to do all the housework and cooking. This idea that women shouldn't have a career, should stay at home and look after it, might have originated from male chauvinism, but then it became the normal thing. A lot of women accepted it. They would dream about men, their wedding day, a white one of course, when they would be a princess for the day. Clearly not all women thought like this, and some women later achieved equality with men, but many did not challenge the accepted order. Olive had been brought up to believe that this is what she would one day want; it was the best thing for her. Consequently, when she didn't get married until she was forty she felt very rejected, a freak that had been left on the shelf.

It was considered unmanly, especially in the 19th century, for a man to do any housework or cooking, and being manly was very important in those days. It created a very big problem when they were old and widowed and needed a helping hand. Olive discovered this when she had been asked to assist someone. It was a thorough nuisance that they found it insulting when it was suggested that they should learn to cook. Yet she couldn't help thinking that senility also played a part. They couldn't have been as silly as that, not even if they were born in 1880, and she remembered them with so much love.

Was it considered manly in those days to fight in a war? She began to go back to the early 1900s, as though she had been a girl then, and she saw in her dream young Ethel, her hair fair and curly again, the beautiful woman who had married her Great Uncle Bert. Ethel was talking excitedly to her about him. Uncle Bert hadn't minded admitting to her, his best girl, that he was scared stiff and she was telling her all about it. It was something that Olive later heard plenty about. He had fought all through the First World War. He had deliberately rubbed dirt into his wounds, hoping to get an infection so he would be sent home. It was a dangerous game. There was no guarantee that they would see a doctor in time.

As Olive dreamed on it all seemed so real to her, as though she was there. She saw a suffragette, a woman called Fiona, and it was making Fiona furious. She would exclaim, 'A woman could so easily train to be a doctor, so why should there be a shortage of them? Why don't they train them and send them out there instead of getting them just to knit socks for them at home, for when they have frostbite in the trenches?'

But Uncle Bert defied all logic, despite his resistance being so low. He was cold and undernourished, and despite the fact that he had deliberately been trying to get an infection, he never got one. He then went home and married Ethel. She'd got him. She had chased him and chased him, starting off before he even left school, and although it was supposed to be the men that chased the women nevertheless it didn't stop her from saying, 'He's mine!'

Olive wondered if these days that would be accepted or would they say she should not think she owned him, just as a man should not think he owns a woman. She remembered in the 1950s when Ann Shelton had been top of the pops with her record about a soldier that had been stationed in Germany: '*Nein nein, Fräulein, that man is mine, although he's across the sea he's mine, he's mine.*'

Surely that was completely different? It could sometimes be healthy in the same way it could sometimes be healthy for a man to refer to a woman as 'my wife'. In the case of Ethel and Bert, they lived happily ever after.

Olive's father had been born in 1909, and he had been far more liberated. He would push her around in a pram although it would make his mother laugh. She was born in 1880. Sometimes a thing can become accepted yet still be unusual enough to look comical, but Olive's father was never one who cared about what people would think.

During the Second World War too, men didn't mind telling girls they were scared stiff. Olive's cousin, Betty, born 1922, told her how she had doted on a young lad called Tony Busby. 'He was so good looking, I would dream about him all the time,' she told her. In 1938, when they were both 16, she said to him, 'Well Tony, it looks like there's going to be another war, what do you think of that?' He told her he was absolutely terrified. He was well aware he would be expected to fight in it, and sure enough he was later shot down while bombing Germany. 'Just one more person that died for our freedom' Betty would say for many years later.

Olive suddenly woke up. She began to think into it deeply as the bus raced along, still on the motorway and still in the dark. There was snow on the trees they were passing. It's strange how some parents seem to condition their kids without realising it. She remembered how in the 1960s, when she was very young and working in a pub, the landlady had gone into the gents' toilet and put up a notice, 'Could gentlemen please act their age?' She was referring to the graffiti on the wall. You didn't see much of that in women's toilets, and her mother told her that in her day it was never seen. Yet during the 1980s she was staying in a hotel which had a bar and a club attached. The manager had been in the ladies and put a notice up. It was about the scribble on the wall, and finished up with, 'After all, you are supposed to be eighteen.'

'That's equality for you' she had thought. 'It used to be the women in the gents' telling the men to act their age, and now the men are going into the ladies' and doing it.' Yet it still struck her as odd. No woman has told her little girl to be equal to the men, to scribble on the walls, yet plenty of parents have told their son not to do it.

Some of this manly nonsense was still with us today, she reflected. Where did it come from? All parents would deny it came from them. People don't know what they believe in until they are faced with it. Even Olive's father had to admit to that. Her parents had to wait some time before her elder sister was conceived. They did tests on her father to see if it was his fault, and a doctor told him it wasn't. He said, 'You've got enough there to populate the whole of Europe' he said.

Her father found he couldn't help mentioning it when out with his mates at the bar that night. Mentioning something like that is bragging.

Why are there more women vegetarians and vegans than men? Olive suspected that it was because it's considered manly to eat meat. Such nonsense! No man would admit to it. Also, vegetarians and vegans have proved to be so much healthier, time and time again. They don't have heart attacks so often, and that's only the beginning. And there was one thing she was quite certain about; women are no kinder than men. It isn't because a woman would be kinder to an animal than a man. A vegetarian is someone who eats no meat or fish, a vegan someone who will eat no dairy products either. A pescatarian is someone who will eat no meat except fish. Olive had come from a family of vegetarians.

Back in the 1800s Manchester had been full of vegetarian restaurants. Her great aunts had done so much of their courting there with her great uncles. They had worn lovely long dresses, which as a small child Olive had always yearned to wear herself one day.

'Olive! We're not having that back again, they're far too inconvenient to get about in!' they would exclaim. Yet in a film she saw, made in 1901, they were jumping on and off the trams as though they were in jeans. In all circumstances, young people have that skip about them.

It isn't true that vegetarians are healthier because they lead a healthier life style in other ways; the scientists have looked into that. These restaurants of the 1800s were one example of it, there was plenty of smoking going on there, and one of them, as well as having a reading room for men also had a smoking room.

As the bus rumbled along Olive wondered how she could be so awake at times and so asleep and dreamy at others. She thought so much about her parents. They had both died some time ago. She wished they could be with her today. They had met when they were nineteen, it was love at first sight, and they had hit it off forever. For a long time Olive thought all marriages were like that, for divorces were rare in her young day.

The parental instinct can be as strong in the male as it is in the female. In fact, sometimes it can be very strong in the man and not there at all in the woman. In Olive's case both her parents had it equally. They lost a daughter of eight. They were devastated. Her father brought the subject up many years later as he lay dying on his death bed.

They had made a dreadful mistake in keeping it a secret from Olive, who was still a little girl at the time, and they also kept it a secret from her that her Aunty Tooty was dead. Maybe they thought it wouldn't matter so much because she was old, but it mattered a lot to Olive. She began to suffer insomnia, and was frequently wide awake in the middle of the night. She could remember how she would hear the old grandfather clock strike, and know that another hour had gone by with no sleep.

Keeping it a secret from her also made her into a dreadful bully. It does this to children sometimes. In the case of Olive, it was her poor little sister she would push about and tease. She would tell her very frightening stories about witches. She later suffered dreadful remorse for it all, but maybe it was too late. Later, her sister would have nothing to do with her.

Although it was a gross error her parents made there, Olive never, in later life, felt any resentment about it. But at the time, as a child, she felt angry towards them. She sometimes wondered if she'd dare to shout it out at them; she wanted to scream it out at the top of her voice.

She would suspect at times that both her great aunt and sister were dead, yet think at others that perhaps they weren't. Maybe one happy day, she'd look out of the window and see old Aunty Tooty walking up the path. She would rush out of the house to greet her, so she hadn't been told a lie after all, and maybe on another happy day her parents would arrive with the good news, 'We're going to the hospital, your sister's coming home'. But that happy day never came.

In fact, one day, when Aunt Tooty's daughter Betty came to see them, after Olive knew her aunt was dead, she made a vicious attack on her. Knowing it would greatly upset her, she started talking about her and making jeering remarks about a photograph she could see of her. 'Look at that, it's Aunty Tooty' she said. She was indeed very angry that she had been left in the dark for so long.

But many years later, when she was filled with such remorse that she had bullied her little sister so much and realised it might have been this that caused it, she could only feel sympathy towards her parents. In fact her mother once made the sweeping statement, 'Children soon get over a death. I was four when my grandfather died.

I felt just dreadful when they told me he was dead, but only for a very short time.'

Maybe that's why she had got over it so quickly, because they had immediately been so open with her about it. They could all cry together.

Maybe it was also her parents' belief that a child would recover quickly anyway, so they made the decision not to torture themselves by telling her. And it was torture for them when she kept asking, 'Where is she? When is she coming home?' When her mother realised she would have to tell her, her father got up and left the room. They were a youngish couple, still in their thirties, devastated at the death of their child, upset about the aunt, completely bewildered by it all, and completely unable to deal with death. How could they also be expected to deal with a bereaved child? So little was known about it in those days and so little help was available.

Her father had stayed in the regular army for quite some time after the war, although Olive saw him quite often as a child. He came out in 1948, when Olive was four. She didn't recognize him as he had been away nine months. She did know that a very nice man had just come in through the door, and she was thrilled. She was rushing round and round like an excited dog. When she started skipping up and down he started skipping with her. Then suddenly she realised who he was - her father. What had confused her was that she had been told he was coming in a plane, but it was a taxi that turned up at the door.

It was a dreadful shame that after a childhood so full of nice men, her life became filled with such evil and misogyny. Some people may think it was innocence that caused the problem; that she wasn't quick enough to see the writing on the wall.

One woman told her, 'If I hadn't got such a good brother I don't know what sort of a mess I'd be in now.' She meant what sort of psychological mess, what sort of a hang up might she have about men. She had had a very bad father.

Olive had her first taste of misogyny before she left school. A youth had thrown a brick at her and no one could understand why. He was interviewed by the headmaster about it. There was mention of the fact that the other teachers might refuse to teach him, and it was also suggested that they should involve the police. They should have done. The school wasn't qualified to deal with it. He needed thoroughly examining by a psychiatrist. Olive also should have had a lot explained to her. If she had known more about this sort of thing she might have been able to avoid other very big problems she faced later in life. They teach such things far more in schools these days.

She was 28 when she had her next big dose of misogyny. Fred, an old flame from her teenage years, came back into her life. Even as a teenager he had been talking about a woman, how badly she had treated him, and Olive just did not know what it was all about. She was completely taken in. Now he was 30. After marrying this woman she had left him and he kept going on about her, saying how cruel she was, as well as making some vicious remarks about his mother. He was also drinking. Olive's heart was full of compassion towards him, yet she did tell him right from the start they were only friends. She tried to get him the help he needed, to see his doctor, to go to Alcoholics Anonymous, but she soon gave in. He was just not trying to help himself.

It was too late. Fred had never understood that they were only friends. He started saying he felt responsible for her, and trying to take control of her life.

He also thought it would be accepted that he was a compulsive tidier. He wouldn't leave things alone in other people's houses. When he told people this as though it was something admirable, they would tell him 'Well you're a damn nuisance with it.' He would always be putting things back in the wrong place, especially in the kitchen. It was something he could never understand, regardless of how much people shouted at him, 'Leave it alone, will yer?'

Other people had to continually put things back to where they belonged. It does seem that someone that wants control it often starts in the kitchen, but that might only have been Olive's experience.

Far worse than that, Fred started getting absurdly jealous of any other man who went near her, often a sign that a man is going to start getting violent. He was also spreading malicious rumours about her. It couldn't have been at a worse time. It was while there was still this dreadful stigma around about spinsters, they'd missed the boat, were left on the shelf. People can be so nasty, and she found it insulting that he was telling people they were engaged. It was a complete fantasy. If people believed that, they would think she was desperate for a man.

Fred started saying the same things about her as he had said about his wife. For example, he said she was 'very hard', and everyone knew she had been soft, soft, soft. It made them wonder what his wife had been like. But they didn't know why he was saying that. She had come into the category of women he feared but needed, and Fred saw both Olive and his wife in the same way as he saw his mother. Very hard.

She started getting depressed in the true medical sense of the word. In those days she didn't even know about misogyny, never mind that it made people ill. It can make a woman suicidal. Sometimes they try it, sometimes they succeed. They are also prone to other illnesses.

CHAPTER 2

Olive continued to keep nodding off as the coach thundered along the motorway. She went right back to when she had first got involved in a suicide case, and she began to dream. She was back in the old house in Hale on the night it had happened and where it had happened. She and her mother had been called out in the middle of the night by the hospital, because Christopher, a friend of theirs, had collapsed. He was the father of an old schoolfriend of Olive's. By the time they reached the hospital he was dead; he had killed himself. His wife Gladys was there. In this case it was the other way about, it was the woman who hated the man. No one could understand why she was like that or why he put up with it. She would criticize and criticise Chris, frequently in a public place, very much showing him up. But on this night, after drinking heavily, he took an overdose, told his wife he had done it, and then went to bed and sat up reading his newspaper and smoking a pipe. She called an ambulance, but he refused to get into it. He even denied taking the overdose. The ambulance men asked her 'Did you see him take it?' but she hadn't.

CHAPTER TWO

An argument broke out. The ambulance men tried to persuade Chris, if only on the grounds that he had had too much to drink, to go down to the hospital and have his stomach pumped, but he started shouting at them, saying that the house was his and they had to get out of it.

They left. About a quarter of an hour later there was a knock on the door and his doctor was standing there. By this time Chris had gone into a coma. They rushed him into hospital immediately, but it was too late; he died shortly after.

It came as bad news to many people that he was dead. They showed no sympathy for Gladys in any way. Yet she came out with things which sounded so natural, and were so out of character for her. It amazed a lot of people. She had never shown any feeling before and wouldn't have had the sense to know how to put it on. Neither would she have cared. It would be an everyday occurrence for her to have everyone in the room glaring at her, telling her what she was not to do or say, and she would just argue that she was right, so why this sudden concern that she seemed to be showing?

'It's the fact that he's dead I don't like' she said. 'I mean, if he was being very naughty, living with another woman, I wouldn't mind so much. You're one person, not two.'

Maybe in private they had had some quiet times. It was something that had been noticed and commented on in another similar case. If only one of them didn't fear and hate the other, you could see how very suited they would be. If only she would stop nagging; but she never left him alone for a second and nagged him to death.

Gladys was also absurdly jealous, giving people shock after shock at what she was implying was going on, and at times people could only double up laughing. For example at the PTA, if her husband and one of the other mothers were both out of the room at the same time, she would angrily suggest that they had deliberately sneaked off and were somewhere alone together.

Gladys once caused a big scene in a restaurant. When she started telling the waitress 'he's mine' the waitress refused to serve them any more or even to go into the dining room. Her husband was so embarrassed that he walked out on her. She then went into the kitchen, and when she could not find this waitress she said it showed they had gone off together. The manager ordered her out, threatening to fetch the police if she didn't leave immediately. He refused to say where the waitress was, though he did try to make it clear that she wasn't with Gladys' husband.

Olive woke up a little before dozing off again. She continued to think on. She had had her next taste of misogyny when she was 30 - John Clough. He had made her ill. They were practically living together. It was in a big and very old terraced house in Hamilton Road in Longsight, yet it was only a two-up two-down, plus a bathroom and kitchen shared by three men. Two of them had the front room upstairs and John had the other. Olive frequently spent the night with him, and they also frequently cooked and ate together. The market in Longsight was just at the top of the road and Olive loved it. It was one of the best markets she'd ever visited, in a students' area.

At first she thought John was just being awkward. There were few people in those days who knew much about misogyny, so she thought things would get better, and in some ways she liked him. She believed that in time she would be able to reason with him. In any case she needed someone to be able to go out with, to socialize with; it can be so difficult at times for a woman to go out on her own, especially to a pub. It's wrong, but such a lot of socializing revolves round drinking, in fact you can be considered a killjoy not to do it.

John loved to make her look small. He especially liked doing it in front of an audience. One day they had been talking about learning to drive a car. She said everyone had the potential to do that. Then she thought about it. She remembered someone she knew and added, 'Well, unless it's someone who is hopelessly neurotic, they may never learn.'

John thought this was screamingly funny. He wanted to ridicule her, and was repeating it to everyone, changing it from what she had actually said. 'Ha ha ha, listen to what she says! She says anyone who can't drive a car is hopelessly neurotic.'

Knowing so little about men that hate women, she believed there might be some point in telling him that she minded him very much doing this, and that if he said it in front of certain people it might cause offence. She didn't realise that this was what he wanted, to cause her embarrassment, to make her look silly, and if he was really lucky to cause a very big row. If he was especially lucky he could make it look as though it was she who had started it.

One day the room was full of people and she was talking to a man called Bernard when John started on her. Olive wanted to sink through the floor; she started to tug on his arm, hoping no one could see, whispering it into his ear, 'Don't! Oh please don't tell that story.' But loudly and clearly, yet again, as though it was a real big joke and she was a real big fool, he said, 'Do you know what she says? She says that anyone who can't drive a car is hopelessly neurotic.'

Bernard laughed and told them, 'Well I must be hopelessly neurotic, because I can't drive.'

No one else appeared to take much notice. Had they heard her pleading with him, crawling and whispering into his ear telling him not to do it? Did they too feel like sinking through the floor and decide it was best not to hear? She didn't know. Would it be drawing more attention to it if she insisted on telling them what she had really said? She was deeply upset. Why had he done that to her? Why did he make this vicious attack on her? It was a great shame she knew nothing about misogyny.

John loved the fact that she couldn't bake cakes. They would be burnt on the outside and not cooked enough on the inside. It gave him a buzz to see her feeling a failure. He once picked up a piece of one and said, 'You know, there's something wrong with this.' Then he started talking about his ex-landlady and how good she'd been at baking cakes. Olive later discovered that he had recently been round to her house and said the same to her. He had told her, 'You can't bake cakes, but I've got a girlfriend and she knows how a cake should be baked'.

It reminded her of a woman she knew called Pat, who had just passed an exam to be an accountant. Her boyfriend, Raymond, honestly didn't like it. Olive had learned with Pat and Raymond that it was better to keep away. He was causing big problems between them, but Olive didn't know at the time that this was a symptom of misogyny and that he didn't want her to have any friends. For example, it was an absolute nightmare trying to phone her, as he would be at the side of the phone the whole time, demanding to know who it was and what it was about, and disagreeing aggressively with it all. He would be dictating to her what she should be doing instead.

John Clough loved to make Olive feel dirty. She had very greasy hair, and he wouldn't let her wash it every day. He said that if she did so it would make it greasier still, and the more she washed it the greasier it would get. Eventually she realised he was doing it on purpose. When she first said to him, 'I'm going to wash my hair every day and that's that' she believed that would be the end of it. But it became a sort of a game with him, a challenge. As another person wrote about misogyny: 'The dominator is his name, controlling women is his game.'

John could see it was seriously upsetting her so he did it more, until eventually she had to give in and she could only wash her hair every week. It made her feel dirty, having to go around with greasy hair such a lot of the time. She believed that if he could see how degrading she was finding it then he would stop it, but he didn't of course. It just made him worse. A misogynist wants a woman to feel degraded, to break her spirit so that he can control her. There was no feeling whatsoever for her.

Another time they went baby-sitting together for a friend of hers, Josie. It was a great help to this friend. She was having trouble with the people next door, so much so that eventually they moved. It had caused them trouble in a big way. At no time did they want any more trouble, but John was prepared to cause it. Olive, never thinking he wouldn't be willing, said, 'Park a little way up the road, Josie's next door neighbours complain about the noise when people drive off.' But he wouldn't do it. Not even after Olive had gone into some detail about how much it was affecting Josie. She said, 'Sometimes she's even gone to spend the night somewhere else.' He told her he had paid his road tax and he was going to park wherever he liked. Unable to face up to Josie with that, she told him she would babysit on her own.

He drove off as though in a rage, though in fact he was enjoying it all. He then turned up at the house a little later as the persuader, something quite common in misogyny; still Olive wouldn't let him in. Josie later said to Olive about it, 'My concern is that you never marry him.' She never asked her to babysit again.

One day Olive had news which might mean she was going to lose her job. The last thing she felt like doing was going to a party. She felt certain she would never be able to hide the fact that she was in such a dither, and more certain still that she would never be able to look in any way cheerful.

She explained this to John. 'Oh please, no one will notice if we don't go, please let us stay in with news like this' she said, but he insisted they went, and dragged her off to the party. Maybe she was beginning to realise he just did not care about her, yet she still didn't know how bad things could get.

When he was ill and arguments started about where he should stay, he was busy starting up a row between two women, her and one called Marion. Olive put the phone down on her, then phoned her straight back to apologize. It was John Clough who was causing it all, in the same way a woman can start a fight between two men.

Then Olive met another man instead of John; a nice man named Simon. She didn't tell him and John about one another, and when they met, in her mother's hall, they had a fight over which of them should go. They both agreed one of them had to, but it wasn't for them to say which, it was for Olive's mother to decide. Then they wouldn't agree which one should phone her up and ask her. She was in Wales at the time.

Olive stood holding onto the telephone wire as they fought over it. Telephones were plugged in in those days and she knew a wire could be pulled out of the wall in a fight. Eventually Simon won, having pinned John up against the wall, and John left. Her mother said later, sounding quite angry about it, 'Well I'm very glad neither of them did manage to get through. I wouldn't have been pleased at all to have received a phone call from two men having a fight in my hall.'

But of course it wasn't about love for Olive. In the case of John he was fighting to keep control, and in the case of Simon, he genuinely wanted to see this man off. Yet it wasn't because he wanted her himself. It was that although they were only having a passing fling, he nevertheless did have some concern for her, and knew there was something very funny about John.

After this John continued his fight to keep Olive. He was also going round to Josie's and had a very sly way of causing trouble. Pretending to have a broken heart, he said he needed someone to talk things over with as regards Olive. Josie's husband was suspicious and reckoned he was after Josie. Both Olive and Josie told him to stop being so daft, but later they thought he might have been right. When Simon heard about it he sent him a message via Olive and Josie, 'Tell him if he wants any help kicking his head in I'll come round.' It was a message that was never delivered, but then if Simon had thought for a second that it would have been, he would never have sent it. It just relieved his feelings to say it.

One chilly evening Olive was on her way home from work, cold and hungry. She dropped in on Josie in order to avoid John, only to find John there. He had guessed she'd do this, so he hadn't waited for her at home. She realised that he just did not care about her.

John knew what he was doing, so she had it out with him. Then, only a few days later when she arrived at Josie's, he was there again, but this time he was willing to get her something to eat. He went into the kitchen and Olive wondered what Josie would have to say about it, as she didn't like other people in there.

'Keep out!' he said to Olive.

'No, it's you who's to keep out,' she told him, and feared it was the beginning of another row. She did leave the room, and thankfully he did too very shortly after with some chips he had bought for her - he'd put them in the oven. It looked as if he had taken some notice of her after all, but later something happened to show he hadn't.

Yet in some ways he continued to try to be the persuader. He made sweet promises about how good he would be to her in future if she would take him back again - very typical of misogyny. The fact that he changed himself back again into the nice man she had first met made it worse. It made her feel sick. In fact she was sick.

When John was being nice, it showed he could be pleasant if he wanted to. It also showed that it was hypocrisy. No one could understand why he wanted a woman in the first place when he'd treat her so badly once he'd got her. In fact she had challenged two other woman-haters about this, saying 'You don't care about that woman, causing her all this trouble.' And in both cases they had just rubbished it, saying that of course they did. Do they believe themselves that they care?

Although she didn't know there was a word for this sort of thing – misogyny - she did know something. She wasn't going to try to keep a man with threats of desertion. She knew what a dreadful time she would have once that man had got her tied.

John believed she had no right to leave him. He was threatening to interfere with the brakes on Simon's car. He said he could never do that as he would never know when she might be in it, but she knew this wasn't true. It wouldn't bother him if he caused an accident and she was injured in it. He might even like it and enjoy the drama, visiting her in hospital and crying because he was 'sorry' for the 'mistake' he had made. Indeed there would have been plenty of drama if that happened. But far more than that, he might be able to get her into his power if he could get her into hospital. Perhaps he'd even be able to paralyze her. Then he would have stripped her of all her self-confidence, and she would be as dependent on him as he had felt on her.

She later read in a psychology book that a misogynist believes that if he makes a woman weak she cannot leave him, so he won't be abandoned. It also said that he wants to be emotionally taken care of. It seems one crazy mix-up of emotions, emotions which finish up in rage, aggression and cruelty, but not love.

When John did eventually go, he told people, 'She has destroyed me.' He was very good at telling a story about her which made her look dreadful, and some people were completely taken in, yet she had done so much to try to please him.

Many years later she met him again. He told her he had two girlfriends; they had only met once but hated each other. It was in a pub and one of the women, Joy, was sitting at a table waiting for him to come back. She looked very miserable. Olive felt certain he was talking to her in order to annoy Joy. She went over to talk to Joy, who told her she had just come out of hospital with suspected appendicitis, although what was really wrong was never established.

That made Olive's blood run cold. She too had been admitted to hospital with abdominal pains when she'd been trying to leave him, and it emerged that Joy had been trying to leave him too.

Olive had wondered at the time if he had done more than try to destroy her, but had he tried to kill her? When she had looked at her diary she had found that she had had these pains every time he had been round to the house. He would have had plenty of access to her food; in fact he had actually done some cooking for her at times or gone out to get some chips. It wouldn't have been difficult for him to put something in the food, and although both Joy and Olive had got a lot better in hospital, the staff didn't know how they had cured them.

'Make certain it's not him that's doing it' said Olive, 'because the same thing happened to me'. Yet at first she had been so naïve. She had not suspected for a minute that anything John was doing was deliberate. It might sound very simple, but she hadn't got a clue the day she was depending on him to give her a lift to the vets that this would be the moment he'd choose to start a quarrel. She very much needed to take a kitten for treatment. So she had to be nice to him, to agree with everything he said, until after she had had the lift.

She was certain he did know what he was doing on the day he told her what he had been saying about her in a crowd. He finished off with 'And Stephanie was there, so I should think she has now completely disowned you'.

As time went by, she realised why she tolerated so much from some people. She remembered dear little Nigel, who she had looked after when he was so badly neglected. Where was he now? Poor little rich boy. What sort of a psychiatric mess was he in now? Would she find him under a bridge sleeping rough? She felt certain that if ever she found him she would never see any fault in him. If there was any horror, it would be hers. If only she had known then what she knew now. But in those faraway days she was not just young; she was a totally untrained nursery nurse.

As she continued to doze she found herself in another house. It was a very big one, almost a mansion. Some people have more money than most people would dream of, and Nigel's parents were among them.

Nigel was five years old. He had been looked after before by an old school friend of hers, Sarah. It had been a good living-in job she'd had. She had the most dreadful parents; In fact her father was suspected of murder. It was his wife who had said he'd done it. A prostitute had been killed, and they never did get the man. Many years later Sarah said, 'My mother was wicked not to report it, he might kill someone else.' But she'd been afraid of what else might come out. It wasn't because she loved him; she hated him. In those days she could have got him hanged.

The mother also suspected her husband had tried to kill her. He had once wired an iron up so dangerously for her to use that she felt it could only be his work. Another time they were together on a high cliff and he kept telling her what a beautiful view there was and trying to get her to go the edge to have a look. She suspected he intended to push her off, yet it didn't make her treat her daughter any better.

She continued not sticking up for her daughter, still afraid of what might come out. She went on allowing him to ill-treat her, and sometimes even supporting him, in particular in turning her out of the house, a place which should have been Sarah's home. In one bedsitter Sarah had to move into, the old man in the next room had made such advances to her that she'd been afraid to go to sleep at night.

A living-in job suited Sarah. She had a lovely attic to share with little Nigel. It was a very small part of the loft and the ceiling sloped steeply, but there was still plenty of room to stand up in. It was at the top of a narrow staircase. They had a bedroom each, and there was a bathroom there. It was all beautifully carpeted and she had her own television.

But Sarah was young, only nineteen, and she didn't want to devote her life to looking after a child. She was engaged to be married, and she wanted to spend time with her fiancé. She could never understand why his mother objected to her going out with him in the evenings if she didn't want to go out herself, but she did. Sarah was defiant. She would go, whether she had permission or not.

Then her big wedding day came. Little Nigel was a page boy at it, dear little Nigel, for both Olive and Sarah knew so little about children in those faraway days. Many things were done very badly. 'Turn back the clock! Give me another chance!' Olive nearly cried out, as she wondered where Nigel was now. Was her husband once treated like that? What made him what he was? No one knew, and he had never been properly examined by a psychiatrist.

So Sarah left after the big wedding, and Olive took her place.

She'd been to the wedding, seen Sarah all dressed up in white, a princess for the day, and Nigel saying goodbye to her. She did not know how traumatizing he was finding it all, how lost and bewildered he was, nor did she think about how damaging it all might one day prove to be.

Later that night she discovered that he was very upset. But how could she deal with it? Her experience with children was so very limited, and in any case she didn't intend to stay there very long. She was planning on going abroad. It was only a temporary job she had taken in the attics.

She was woken up at midnight that night by Nigel's crying. He was also being sick. Still half asleep, she stumbled out of bed and gently asked him what the matter was. He was crying for Sarah. 'She's going away and I am never going to see her again' he sobbed.

She tried to soothe him by saying, 'You've got me instead'. He looked up at her wide-eyed and full of hope, but then he asked her for how long. She had to tell him she would only be staying a very short time. She took him into her bed and he slept the night there.

The next night the same thing happened, only this time his father heard him. He came up the stairs sounding most distressed, saying 'Nigel, dear me, whatever is it?'

He went to get Mrs Bennett, Nigel's mother, up. She was dreadfully lazy and never did any work. She thought she was a cut above everyone else, or at least the workers, and had no natural feeling for the boy. Yet Mr Bennett had got her out of bed at Nigel's big moment of need.

Olive also got up, went into the room to show willing, but stayed in the background when she saw that they were dealing with it. But now, many years later, she wondered how she could have been so hard. There were so many other things she should have seen to, yet she was afraid of leading him on. How dreadful to make him promises and then not keep them! Oh, if only she could turn back the clock! Now she would make them, and make certain they were kept. She wished she had assured him she would do her best to keep in touch. She could have promised to be his pen pal, and said she would always be in contact with Sarah for him. There was so much she would have spoken to Sarah about, if only she had known then what she knew now.

His name was down for a boarding school when he was eight. She thought it was very hard when he was so keen on his home. Someone said when they heard how neglected he was, 'he'll grow up no good.' If Olive had properly understood what the words 'no good' meant, she would have made a lot more effort to find out more. Now she knew what it was like to be in the hands of someone who is just a nuisance to everyone, who has to be locked up in a police cell, and when they are dead no one is sorry to hear about it.

It was unbelievable that Mrs Bennett thought she was superior, when in fact she was totally useless. There was a housekeeper living in, an elderly lady called Mrs Longton, who had four small rooms attached to the side of the house; in fact you could almost call it a separate house. She saw to everything. Olive had felt that by staying and helping she was encouraging a parasite, Nigel's mother. Now she wouldn't have let that bit bother her, yet even then, she wondered if in those circumstances it was different. If there was something really wrong with the woman, and if Nigel was so much in need, should that change everything, all her views on it?

On Olive's first day Mrs Bennett told her she would have to wear an overall, and although Olive didn't mind, it was rather like dressing her up as a servant. She also said she would always have to wear shoes. This was a big blow to Olive; she had deformed feet, and sometimes had to leave her shoes off. It disgusted her that with this woman's little boy so upset at the change of a nanny, her only concern seemed to be in keeping the new one in order. She had to show that she was on top. She made a tremendous commotion about Olive not wearing shoes, but she didn't appear to be bothered about anything else.

Nigel too had been leaving his shoes off, and Mrs Bennett told him, 'I think I know what's been making you vomit, you've been going around in bare feet.' Olive thought to herself, 'My God, you've got no brain!' Olive had heard that going barefoot can cause a cold. Such nonsense, but it was the first time she'd heard it can also make you sick.

Every evening, Olive would wait outside the dining room while Mrs Bennett served supper. Mrs Bennett would then come out and give her her dinner. She would say, 'My goodness me, you do look smart in your shoes and overall!' It was condescending. Yet at times she did seem to be trying. She had paid for the overall; it was a very nice one that Olive had chosen for herself at an overall shop in Cross Street, Altrincham. His mother was never mean with money. You could always borrow a bit from her if you spent your wages too soon.

It continued to amaze Olive how Mrs Bennett thought she was superior. For example, she wouldn't let Nigel play with the local children, although they were in no way rough. He asked her why and she couldn't answer. But the answer came when the mothers of one of these 'rough' little children snubbed her. Mrs Bennett explained to Nigel, 'They turn their noses up at us.'

She was treating the place as though it was an institution more than a home. Olive only had two half days off a week, never a whole day, but a lot of the time she was lounging about while he was at school, so she could hardly call herself overworked. She liked it that way. On one of her half days she had to go straight out, so she left her dinner to be put in the oven for when she came back. However, she was told she was not allowed to do that.

Nigel's mother didn't look after him, not even when it was Olive's half day off. He would go to the gardener's house instead. His wife would have him and give him his tea. Mrs Bennett would consider it a real problem if anything happened that meant that she had to have him. The housekeeper couldn't understand it as she had so enjoyed bringing up her two boys. She told Olive how once when Mrs Bennett was crying, she said she'd look after Nigel. Mrs Bennett had turned round and still with tears on her face said 'Why should you?'

The housekeeper had thought, 'Yes, why should I?' But she didn't say it. She just said she would. The power of tears can do a lot.

No one could understand why Mrs Bennett minded going to school to meet him. He would so look forward to seeing her and then she wouldn't turn up. The first time Olive went she was completely unaware of this. When he asked 'Is Mummy at home?' she said 'Yes', thinking she was. When he arrived there and found that she was out, he was furious. He went storming into every room looking for her and then came out with three or four words to describe her. All of them most people would agree with. One was 'useless', but where did he get it from? Olive knew enough about children to know a child of five would never be able to sum things up and judge it so well. He must have heard someone else say it.

Then Nigel started on Olive. 'You told me she was in!' he shouted angrily. She knew he was right. She sat on the stairs, lifted him onto her knee and told him how sorry she was about it, and that she did not realise how very important it was to him. After that, whenever she went to meet him, knowing it would be the first question he'd ask, she would always check where his mother was before she came.

But far more than that, he would hope that his mother herself would come. Olive didn't like it that the sight of her was a disappointment to him. Sometimes his mother had promised to collect him, and then she would change her mind and say, 'Sarah, you go.' Perhaps it was because she enjoyed her position of authority and believed in keeping the workers in their place.

If Olive ever wanted to go out in the evening and it wasn't her half day, she had to say, 'Please may I go out, Mrs Bennett?' Yet she'd had trouble keeping girls, she was afraid of losing them, and Olive never felt afraid of challenging her on anything if she went over the top.

Some of the girls had played the dirty on her in a bad way. One girl who had applied for the job had accepted her fare there and been sent her ticket, paid for by Mrs Bennett, and then not turned up for the interview. She just came up to Manchester to have a day out.

She would sometimes be very happy because at long last she thought she had had found someone who seemed suitable, and then the references would come through and they were dreadful. She never quite got one which said, 'Just out of prison for abusing children', but that was about the only comment she didn't get.

So she was very pleased when Olive turned up. If only she would stay. Little Nigel had talked a couple of times to Olive about marrying her one day. Now, so many years later, she knew how afraid he must have been of being abandoned. He imagined that if he married her when he was grown up he could be certain he would have her for ever. She laughed and said, 'Nigel, when I'm forty and you're twenty-one, you won't want to marry me!'

Now she wished she had said she would, if he still wanted to at that age. It would at least have made him feel secure. She'd have kept in touch. And indeed she'd have been quite safe there, for at 21, marriage to a woman of 40 would have been the last thing he'd have wanted.

The housekeeper told her his mother had no natural love for the boy, something that Olive had already noticed. When he had been small, he would sit upstairs in his cot and hardly anyone would go up to see him. He was a long time learning to talk, maybe because he was spoken to so little. Then he had a trained nanny, a very good one, for months; she was 40 and it was she who got him really talking. A dreadful shame she left.

Yet although so much was so bad, he was nevertheless born into a world where it went unsaid that people were pleasant. A man's place is in the kitchen if his little boy is in it and needing him. That was where his father was. Would it be a coincidence that he'd be making himself a cup of coffee at precisely the right moment?

One day Nigel was talking about Teddy on the pot. Olive thought it was a bit much. His father exclaimed, 'Nigel, don't be so disgusting! People are having their breakfast.'

After this he appeared to be lost for words, 'Nigel! I mean!' Olive sat there giggling. Mr Bennett was faking shock as he continued to make himself a cup of coffee. No one could have cared less than Nigel did. He wasn't at all bothered that he had shocked his father.

Another time workmen were outside the house digging a hole in the road. Nigel was curious and went outside to look. When morning tea break came up for them they knocked on the door to see if they could have their tea caddy filled up with hot water. It couldn't be done, because at that particular moment something needed doing to the kettle or the plug. Nigel overheard the housekeeper referring to it as a nuisance. Nigel started going out to them again, but his father stopped him. He told him that you leave the word 'nuisance' out of a sentence when you're making someone a cup of tea. He said you have to very politely say, 'Could you wait a minute? It will be done as quickly as possible.'

Then Nigel came back. They'd gone to the house next door for their tea. His father said, 'Well it seems they have realised they chose an inconvenient moment.'

This was a very good demonstration of the importance of being pleasant. It was very different from the way it is for some deprived children. His father didn't say, "it's a good joke this is, you'll get no cup of tea from us" and the workmen didn't say, "Give us a cup of tea or we'll beat you up".

As the coach went along, Olive comforted herself with things like this. She thought about far worse cases than little Nigel. For example, a child who was in his cot all day and dreaded hearing footsteps coming up the stairs, because he was so used to beatings. Nigel didn't hear footsteps often enough. He was neglected, but when he did hear footsteps it would always mean something nice. No one ever went up that narrow staircase to the attic unless it was to see him.

As years went by she would hear more. One example was the hanging of Saddam Hussein. Saddam left the world as he came into it, with people shouting at each other and doing their best to insult one another. In the last few seconds before he died he and the hangmen had a slanging match over what sort of a Muslim you should be. From the day he was born until the day he was hanged it was the language he was used to, and when he was a child he had lived in fear of his stepfather's beatings. Is there a connection, or is it a coincidence that Adolf Hitler had also lived in fear of his father's beatings?

The subject of death troubled little Nigel, but it was something Olive felt completely unable to deal with. When he came to the bit, 'People would cry if I died' she felt something needed saying. He was more than frightened of dying; he was afraid no one would care if it happened. But the housekeeper was there. She hastily assured him that people would certainly cry.

'Nigel, you mustn't say such things,' she said. 'The thought of it is so upsetting. The whole house would stand still, the clock on the wall would stop ticking, people would pass one another on the stairs and not speak if you died.' Clearly she had been in a house where there'd been a bereavement. She also told him it was so rare for a child to die that it wasn't worth worrying about.

CHAPTER 3

Olive wanted to see what it was like to fly, so she flew to Italy to work. The first family she stayed with had quite a large first-floor flat, with the grandmother living on the ground floor below. The children were dreadful; they howled the whole of the time and the woman she worked for, known simply as Signora, was well used to servants. They had a young married couple living in and waiting on them. Signora thought it was only right that she should do no work.

Olive arrived just at the beginning of December. It was a complete washout as the two little girls, aged five and two, did not accept her and only wanted their own mother or the nanny they had had before. They also refused to eat. This wouldn't have mattered if the mother had just left them to it until they had an appetite again, but she would stand at the end of the table saying, 'Come on, eat, eat!' The two children would sit in front of their food piled high, not even picking up the spoon to begin.

At first Signora was quite pleasant to Olive, wanting to get on with her, but this didn't last long. She began to blame her for everything that went wrong, and she would get worked up into an excited state.

Olive found that the Italian middle classes were the same as any other class anywhere at all; they varied a lot. She was not the only one who was shocked at how rude some of the children could be, and how the parents would not take it seriously. They would say things to the au pair like, 'You shut your face.' The first time it happened, Olive, not understanding the language very well, did not know how bad it was. She was once in the park larking about with some youths and she said this to one of them. They were half amused and half amazed, and asked her, 'Where did you get that from?' When she told them, they pointed at the big house on the hill. Looking amused, they said, 'In that big, posh house there, you learnt that?' They all burst out laughing.

However there was many a middle-class Italian family who would not only take it quite seriously if a child of theirs said that, but would feel they had failed.

In this first family she stayed with, the woman was so mean with money that Olive wondered if she had some sort of insecurity if she didn't hang onto every penny. She first realised this after she had taken the two little girls out for a walk. A dog was jumping up at them and clinging to them in a way that was very frightening. Olive had to pick up the two-year-old and hold her high above her head while the dog jumped up at her instead, but at times the dog seemed determined to jump up only at the child. She was howling for her mother. People passing by helped by chasing the dog away. When Olive got back, she felt traumatized, but her Italian was nothing like up to explaining what had happened. None of them could speak English. She had no need to worry. The child just gabbled on and on about it, saying in Italian 'Oh Mummy it was dreadful' and explaining everything. Olive could understand that much.

Then Signora asked where the child's glove was. 'The dog ran off with it' she told her. This was not accepted as an excuse at all. She pointed a finger straight at Olive and said, 'You are supposed to be looking after things like that.'

Olive was able to ask her in Italian which was more important, the glove or the child, and although she took the point, she nevertheless remained quite adamant about the glove and continued to complain about it. She said she should look after them both. It was unbelievable.

Still feeling in a complete turmoil about it all, Olive went away to make herself a cup of coffee. The woman came into the kitchen and told her to get on with her work. Olive promised she would do it in ten minutes, but she was going to have her drink first. She needed something to help her recover. This wasn't good enough for the woman and she said she should start her work straight away, it wasn't coffee time. Olive refused, so Signora went into the next room and sat there sulking about it for quite some time. She was very upset about the glove, and about Olive's coffee break. Nor did she show any gratitude to the many people who rallied round helping.

Olive wondered if people only noticed when the rich were mean, because poor people could be just as bad. She had met someone on social security who wouldn't give two pence towards a box of matches, although he used them when he smoked and the money was going towards a famine in Africa and there had been a lot of publicity about it. She said, 'These Third World countries are not going to accept that we've got all the food, they're going to revolt'. He made a joke about how poor he was and how they couldn't possibly revolt against him. He reminded people at times of Marie Antoinette and 'Let them eat cake'. She told him he was going to get his throat cut.

Several people had said about the rich, 'That's how they've made their money, by being so mean.' That would be a simple explanation and one that made sense, yet Olive didn't think so. She had met people who had lost all their money because they were so grasping and wouldn't pay for anything. No one would deal with them. She had also met people, several of them, who had worked for some very rich people yet were not at all mean.

Before Olive started this first job in Italy she was told she'd have a bedroom to herself and in a sense she did, although the family had cupboards in it with all their clothes inside and they frequently went in to get them. One day the husband came in when she only had her petticoat on. However, he immediately retreated with big apologies, calling her 'Signorina', almost the equivalent to Madam in English if it is emphasized in the way he did. It was at a time when he would not have expected her to be there, and he never did it again.

She did start getting stroppy when the aunt arrived and they put her in the other bed in her room. After Olive objected the bed was moved out and put into the children's room instead. Then, at Christmas time, in a row about the children refusing to eat, Olive gave notice to leave.

On New Year's Eve she went out for a walk. She came in late and the grandmother came out of her ground floor flat into the hall and invited her in. She gave her a drink of sherry. She told Olive about her daughter-in-law upstairs, that she was too agitated, and indeed Olive knew this, she had heard her shouting and kicking things around. She and the grandmother saw the New Year in together.

Olive left early one morning shortly after; it was chaotic getting away, she thought she'd never make it. For one thing Signora resented her going, but apart from that, the children were being their usual screaming selves, milk was being spilt everywhere, so it was more of a question of what wasn't going on than what was. A railway station was peaceful to her compared with that. But even then, with not being able to speak Italian very well it was a nightmare to make certain she was on the right train. When at last she was on it she fell asleep. She woke up in perfect peace, finding she was the only person in the carriage and she was high up in the mountains with snow falling everywhere. She was on her way to join another family in Cortina who were on a skiing holiday. They were a very rich family. The children were lovely, and she met other au pair girls and mothers.

One woman told her a story which made her think. Because she had been asked to act as a go-between, as she could speak both Italian and English, she had talked to a family on the phone. The au pair working for them was very unhappy. The conversation was a little cold, and then eventually this woman lost patience and snapped, 'Well what I have understood is, she was told she could have a room of her own and she doesn't have one'.

She said she didn't know how many people were on the other end of the line but she was most certainly shouted down. The whole lot of them were practically shrieking, 'She HAS got her own room!' There was a tremendous amount of indignation and the Signora had an army to defend her. This go-between just couldn't understand it because this girl had so very clearly said she didn't have her own room. Olive wondered if it was a case of what you consider your own. Is it your own room if people like Aunty are going to be put up in the spare bed there?

Olive remembered Nigel. When the television hadn't been working in his parents' sitting room, his father had asked Olive if he could watch hers. Nigel especially wanted to watch something and of course he was in her room all the time, yet his father still understood that this shouldn't be taken for granted.

The new children in Italy were a girl of four called Nicoletta and a boy of two called Antonio. They were very well behaved and started learning to speak English very quickly. It was amazing how fast children would learn. The parents and grandparents would jump with joy when they heard it. One day Olive said to the two-year-old, 'Do you know where my handbag is?' and he started running away to get it. The grandmother, not understanding English, shouted 'Come back here, don't run away when people are speaking to you.' When Olive explained it to her and he returned with the handbag, the grandmother was overwhelmed with joy.

Another time they went into a shop together and Antonio started chasing a dog around, speaking in English. The shop assistant, thinking he was English, thought this was very sweet. She shouted across to the other girls, 'Hear this, can you hear this kid here? Listen to his English.' And they all started going 'Oh isn't he sweet' when suddenly he came out with a mouthful of Italian. That made them sit up.

'He can speak Italian!' They exclaimed. Then, thinking that he was English, and that Olive was his mother, they said, 'Signora, you do know don't you, your little boy's Italian is very good?' In fact it was his English that was very good.

When Olive first went to Italy she heard a mother explaining something to her little girl. Olive's Italian was good enough to be able to understand what she was saying. It was, 'It's not everyone who can speak Italian. Some people can't.' The child looked bewildered. Every time Olive walked across the room the child's eyes were on her. 'What a funny woman, she can't speak Italian.'

After two months the skiing holiday was over and they went back to their house in the north of Italy. It was the biggest she'd ever seen. Again it shocked Olive, first the way the woman never did any work and then how superior she thought she was. There was no consideration for the servants, which was very different from Mrs Bennett in England.

They had two people coming in working during the day, one of them full-time, and there was also a full-time manservant living in. It amazed Olive that he put up with so much, but did he think he'd lose a living if he didn't? The hours they worked astounded other Italians, especially communists. They found it unbelievable, and Olive would say to them, 'I'm sorry to sound so arrogant but I know more about your country than you do.' They told her it was all illegal and also, with great certainty, that it wasn't going to last much longer. 'They are in for a rude awakening' they said.

For example, the living-in manservant didn't have a day off. He was supposed to have two half days a week. That was just for a few hours, and he would be expected back in the evenings. But every time, just when he was about to go off in the early afternoon, something would come up which would stop him going until later. It became more and more obvious that Signora was doing it on purpose. She must have resented him having time off.

When she had guests in, he couldn't go off until they'd left and sometimes that would be quite late, even if there was nothing to do. It wouldn't be that they were business acquaintances or anyone they would want to impress. He had to hang about the hall just in case a light needed switching on.

When they had gone skiing they had taken one of the women servants with them to live in, a woman called Teresa who usually only came in during the day when they were at home. Just when she was about to finish one evening, having worked all day, Signora invited some guests for supper. They had popped in that afternoon. She was pressing it - 'Oh, do stay.' How very kind of her, except that it wasn't her who would have to do all the work. She only had to pay for the food, and she had such a lot. Teresa didn't get any overtime and she now had to start a meal for a party of six.

On top of things like this, Signora would frequently be grousing away at Teresa; nothing was good enough for her. One day she said to her when she was serving her some food at the table, 'It takes patience with you'. And the little girl of four stroked the servant's arm and said, 'Oh poor Teresa'. It should have made her mother feel very ashamed. Teresa was very touched by it and she and Olive agreed in privacy that she was a lovely child, they should have more patience with her, but the point was they didn't want her, not all the time. Like any other kid, she was forever under their feet.

It did once get back to Signora, when they were preparing for a dinner party for twelve, that a servant had said there was a lot to do in the kitchen. She rubbished it and said there wasn't. Olive realized that this was ignorance, as she had never done any work herself and another person commented, "OK then, if there's not much to do then swap jobs for a year".

It was very strange the way Signora didn't like the manservant watching the television while she was out, even though he was expected to stay in and look after the place. Olive noticed that if he was watching something, for example football, something he was very keen on as were many Italians, he got very nervous every time she walked past the door. She went in to give him assurances that she wouldn't report what he was doing to anyone. Later on Signora had reason to be suspicious; Olive told her a big lie, very firmly saying, 'No, I've never seen him watching it.'

Then she received bad news about Nigel. Things weren't going well there at all and his father had left his mother. Poor little Nigel, he now came from a broken home. It reminded her that she had once woken up there in the middle of the night and thought, 'I'd better be careful here.'

She remembered a case long ago where a man killed his wife and then the servant girl, because the servant had witnessed something. Olive realised it was a silly thing to be thinking about, but when she arrived at breakfast next morning, the housekeeper told her Mr Bennett had got up in the middle of the night and gone away for a few days.

'I wonder if they had a row?' the housekeeper said. Yet it was only now, when Olive heard he had actually left her, that she wondered if she had heard something and this was why she'd woken up thinking this.

But now she was far away in Italy and had other things to deal with. There was a myth that it was bare feet and low temperature that cause a cold. She was also told it could cause pneumonia. It nearly drove Olive mad and made her wonder what she believed. There were other myths she noticed, for example that milk straight out of the fridge is bad for the stomach. Some of these people had too much time and they made work with it, just as long as it wasn't work for them. Olive did write a list of many things and wished she'd kept it; it was quite a long one.

How pious it is to always be clean and have everything beautifully ironed, if it isn't you who has to do the ironing and washing. Signora would leave things out to be ironed when they didn't need it at all.

The husband could be as bad, and that surprised Olive, as he most certainly knew what work was. One day an apple had gone brown because it had been peeled and cut up too soon. It hadn't been peeled for very long, it was still perfectly healthy to eat and only mattered if you didn't like the colour of it. Yet he still told them to make certain it didn't happen again. Olive thought this was terribly bad for children, to let them think that they should be treated with such care when there was so much poverty and so many needy cases about.

Another time on a beautiful summer's evening he touched the

little girl's arm and asked her if she was cold. They had this thing about the cold. Olive thought, 'Oh don't work her up!' But he kept on, eventually saying, 'Yes or no, are you cold?' So she said she was. They then asked the manservant who was waiting on them to go into the kitchen and get the cook, who would be busy preparing the meal, to go upstairs and get her cardigan for her. The cook did this and then gave it to the manservant to bring into the dining room for her. What a performance! What a team to have working for you and on something so unnecessary! Some people would have called her a spoilt little brat, and yet she was a lovely child. Maybe though, more unbelievable still was how the children were always made to wear a vest regardless of how hot the weather was, and this was in Italy where the weather was very hot. They even had to wear it when one of them had a heat rash.

If they went to the seaside there would be a performance on the beach. After the children had been swimming, there was one big rush to dry them down as though every second counted.

This family believed the home was all-important. They didn't believe in boarding schools. They wouldn't let them go into hospital to have their tonsils out until it got so that they had no choice. Before then they'd had some very bad nights with the children crying with sore throats. They didn't take them to the doctor's, he came out to see them. That included the specialist.

Although in so many ways they were a very nice family, Olive nevertheless got tired of them and went to Rome. She found some of the Italian men absolutely dreadful. She heard a horrendous story from two other girls who had been on a couple of journeys from Venice. The first time they went, when the conductor looked at the girls' ticket he stroked her arm. 'Don't touch her, there's no need to touch!' said the other girl to him. He took great offence at this, and later during the journey he came up to them, started ranting and caused the most dreadful scene. They decided to forget it, but the next time they went exactly the same thing happened. This time it was for nothing; the girl hadn't even said to him, 'Don't touch'. They had to sit to attention through the whole journey, for he said he had to keep his bus in order.

The girl's employers, Italians, put in a complaint against him. His defence was that he had to keep his bus looking decent and they had been lounging about. It implied that they'd been doing things like showing a lot of leg when putting their heads down on the next seat to have a sleep. It had been very late at night and at a time when a lot of the passengers were doing the same. Later, when these two girls knew more about psychology, or at least about misogyny, they realised how serious it could be. Sometimes these men finish up by seeing all women as prostitutes and even killing them.

Fortunately nothing like this happened to Olive on her journey to Rome. She stayed with several families, but the first chucked her out practically the day she arrived, for nothing. There had been no disagreement. This left her in a dreadful mess as she had nowhere to go and knew no one. Then she discovered a place called 'Protection to the Young', run by nuns. She could go out to work every day from there and earn enough to keep herself, or at least pay for her board and keep. She did housework for a private family and helped to teach the daughter to speak English. At the hostel she slept in a dormitory full of girls and ate at set times in a dining room full of people. There were all nationalities there and they all swapped notes on various things that had happened to them.

She soon got fed up with it and wanted a living-in job. She got one straight away but it only lasted a day because the husband made a pass at her. That explained why so many other girls had left so suddenly. Signora seemed completely unaware that he was doing this, but she complained at the same time about girls never staying, saying

'I don't know what it is I am doing wrong'. Olive thought she'd better tell her, and she left Signora nearly crying.

In fact, throughout Olive's time in Italy, and despite so many of the men being so awful, that was the only time anything like this happened. In the other families she had stayed in, the husbands had always been most respectful. Yet some of the other men in some parts of Italy were dreadful enough to make it impossible for a woman to be able to go out on her own. It took away their freedom. Women have said they'd had their holidays just wrecked by men who wouldn't go away when they were told to. It wasn't nice, good-looking men who were doing it but often men of a most unsuitable age. They didn't seem to realise that a girl is most unlikely to want someone with an age gap like that.

How many men do we pass in the street every day? If one in a hundred is going to follow us around, refuse to go away, then it's not going to be long before you've got a problem. Whether or not it would be true to say that the rest of them are just shy young men Olive didn't know, but still there is many an Italian who has to pluck up courage to ask a woman out. Lots and lots of them.

It was certainly safe for Olive to go back to the hostel, and true to its name, it gave 'protection to the young.' No man was going to get in there. One girl said when she saw how careful the nuns were when opening the door, 'They're so afraid a man is going to burst his way in.' Olive laughed. Yet it didn't take her long to realise that if they didn't always do that it wouldn't be long before one did.

She did eventually find a living-in job with a nice family. It was to a lord and lady, who had the most impossible teenage daughter, Barbara, although maybe she was no more than typical. At times they seem to pick on their fathers a lot and the motto seems to be, 'Let's get Dad going.' She certainly had a lot of success in winding up her father, Lord Marconi. She managed to get him to chuck his dinner up the wall. Olive went to get a broom and shovel to clear up the mess, while Lady Marconi had hold of his arm, trying to calm him down, but agreeing with him at the same time that there had never been a man in Rome with a more impossible daughter than he had. Olive was trying to calm Lady Marconi down by getting hold of her arm and trying to get her to listen, saying that although this may be true there had once been a man in England with a teenage daughter who was worse, that was herself when she was 14. Lord Marconi found this totally unacceptable, and shouted loud and clear, 'There's never been a man anywhere on earth with a daughter as impossible as mine!'

Olive continued to sweep up the pieces from the floor while his wife continued to soothe him with, 'I know darling'. She paused only to scowl at Barbara and say, 'You are NOT to do this!'

Olive then began to clean the wall where his dinner had landed. Unfortunately that only showed how dirty the rest of the wall was.

Nothing as bad as that happened again and things went smoothly along for months. The only thing the parents did begin to complain about was the way Barbara was always on the phone. She was always talking to her friends even though she saw them all day at school, and the bill was horrendous. She should have been getting on with her homework.

One day Olive had just stepped out of the bath when she saw Lord Marconi getting out of a taxi outside. He had come home from work unexpectedly early. The bathroom led off the hall and she knew Barbara was on the phone in the room just across the way. Olive very quickly put some clothes on, then stood at the bathroom door shouting across the hall, 'Watch out, here comes your father!'

Barbara immediately put the phone down. Then they met in the hall and had a shock. He was standing there. However had he managed to get up those steps and inside the house so quickly? He had heard Olive shouting 'Watch out, your father's coming in.' He had heard the bell of the phone go down, and then he had heard them both gasp in horror when they saw him. He just stood there motionless, making no comment at all. Olive did wonder later though if she had done more good than harm showing herself up as a comrade of his daughter.

They were a nice family, but Olive still wanted to move on. The next family she went to owned a restaurant and had lots of money, and they too had a teenage daughter, Suzanne, who was very good at winding up her father. It happened during a discussion on what to do about criminals. It might have seemed to some people that she and her father had completely different views on it, and it might have seemed to others that she was making it up to get him going. That week in Rome two men had gone into a jeweller's shop and shot dead the owner's two sons right in front of him. They got one of the men straight away, but it set the whole of Italy looking for the other one. They knew who he was, but they had to find him. It was on the front page of every newspaper and everybody was rejoicing when they got him.

This was when Olive first realised how good her Italian was becoming. First she understood the news on the radio, despite the fact that they talk so fast, and then she leaned out of the window and shouted it down to someone, 'They've got him!' Several Italians turned round in the street to rejoice and to check up that they had heard right.

Suzanne's father asked her, 'And what am I expected to do if a man comes into the restaurant and shoots you and your sister dead in front of me?' She told him he should go to court like a true Christian and ask for forgiveness for the two men who had done it. That made him angry. He went very red in the face and stood up holding his dinner plate, as if he was going to chuck it up the wall, 'I should do WHAT?' he shrieked.

His wife rushed forward, and in a struggle she managed to get the plate out of his hand. He then stormed out of the room, slamming the door behind him with the most almighty bang. His wife followed, doing her best to calm him down. But she pointed a finger directly at Suzanne and said, 'You are to stop this!'

The nuns in Italy were nothing like those Olive had heard about in Ireland or even in England. They were nice. She'd been told that in Ireland and Britain they were so strict as to be cruel. Suzanne and Barbara in Italy were taught by the Italian ones. Olive used to go to the school sometimes to give private tuition to someone in English. They let her have a room there. They also lent her a lot of English novels. Maybe because she was away from her country, she loved to read them so much. And frequently she would be in the cloakroom at home time, all of them larking about including the nuns, and of course, they would like her being there, someone to lark about with the girls in English.

While staying with this family she found out something very bad about another family, and how dreadful it was for the English girl who stayed with them, a girl called Linda, who had been in the hostel at the same time as Olive. Linda had been introduced to them by another girl staying in the hostel called Pat, and Pat seemed to hate all Italians, or maybe she simply hated humanity. She said that Rome was a wicked city, called all the men something rotten, and then went on to talk about their wives. She said that all Italian women were very strict and seemed at times to be excusing the men for being what they were with a wife like that.

She would be saying other extremely bad things about the women at the same time. It was all absolute rubbish. No one could understand why she didn't go back to her own country if she hated them all so much. She had been in five families in a month. Everywhere she went there was trouble.

For one thing she said that the Pope was a homosexual. The Italians burst out laughing when she said this. This was before there was a lot of publicity about what some of them had been up to, and they did know that it wasn't unheard of for a Catholic priest to have a mistress on the side. Of course there's all the difference between a homosexual and a paedophile; it is with paedophiles that people come down so heavily, and it's a wonder that Pat didn't say this about him. It is thought she deliberately got this girl, Linda, a job in a very bad family in order to prove her point that all Italians are dreadful. And indeed the point was proved, if this one was the only one to go by. For example she was supposed to have a day off a week, but she wasn't getting it, and when she did finally have a day off scheduled she was woken up at six o'clock in the morning to be told the baby was crying.

They then all went away to stay in a house by the sea for the summer, taking Linda with them, although it hadn't been a part of the agreement at the interview. In fact the first she heard of it was when she was woken up in the morning and told they were going. She hated it there. It was non-stop work, the child was dreadful, howling the whole of the time, and she was out of contact with all of her friends. The couple tried to keep Linda's whereabouts a secret from Olive, and Olive believed she really had left without telling them and didn't mean to threaten them when she told the husband she would have to report her missing to the police. He stayed in Rome much of the time. When she made this threat, he gave her the address. She was quite upset to realise that he had known where Linda was all the time.

Also taking a keen interest in all this was a young man called Louis, who spoke very good English. He met her on the beach and was very blunt with her. When she first started telling him she could never see him because she was working all the time, he wondered if that was just an excuse. He said, 'Are you telling me to piss off? Because if you are then I'll piss off, but if not I'll help you get away from them and then I'll piss off.'

He met Olive in Rome and Linda's escape was planned for the next day. He would give her a lift to wherever she wanted to go. She had everything packed, but of course her plan was not to be made too obvious. On the beach, with Louis standing by her side, she told the woman she was going. There was the most tremendous commotion. She wished she'd just slipped out of the back door and left a note. A crowd gathered to see what was going on, one of them a nun. At one stage the woman was pulling on her arm, trying to physically keep her, while Louis had hold of her other arm to pull her the other way. Then a woman came forward who could speak English. She told her, 'This woman is telling us he is kidnapping you and she is rescuing you.' Linda cried out, 'It's the other way about, she's kidnapped me and I'm being rescued by him!'

The rest of the crowd didn't trust this woman's English and someone else had to confirm it - yes, she had understood it quite correctly. Linda had said this.

Linda then went to stay with an elderly lady in Rome, Signora Ugolini, a school teacher coming up to retirement. She taught English but wasn't good at it herself. She was very glad to have someone English staying in the house with her. She also taught German, a subject she was really good at, but that was another class and none of the children were interested. She had to make them do some work, which at times could be quite a struggle. But in her English class they were all most enthusiastic.

She was afraid of what they might ask her in case she didn't know. One day there had been an earthquake. She phoned up Olive to ask how you say 'earthquake' in English, as she was certain they would ask her next day at school. Olive went round to the flat, buying an English paper at a stall on the way, with reports about the earthquake. Together they went through it, and Signora Ugolini took it to school with her next day.

Signora Ugolini had had a sad life. She had suffered polio as a child and had always resented the terrible limp it had left her with. She married very young, soon had a baby boy, and her husband had then left her and gone off with a French woman. He always kept in touch with his son. Then when the son grew up he went to live with his father in Paris. This wasn't because he preferred him, but simply that he was working in Paris, and he found it very convenient that he had someone there who could give him some accommodation.

His mother didn't like it, but she was always thrilled to hear from him. One day when Olive was in the flat, and she picked up the phone, thinking it would be a routine call from work, she suddenly exclaimed, 'Darling, where are you?'

It was a phone call right out of the blue. He was in Rome. Olive knew it was time for her to go. She knew she would only want to be with him.

Signora Ugolini, although she was elderly, did have a man friend. He was living with her for a while, but then she chucked him out. Why had she chosen him in the first place? He wasn't her type. For a start he was lazy, and that was something she couldn't bear. He wouldn't help with the housework. He would talk about the kitchen being a mess, although he hadn't got a job and had all day to clean it himself. Even in those days, in Italy, all Italians that heard about it were horrified. The men weren't like Olive's old uncles, born 1880 in Britain, the men who would feel unmanly if expected to do any housework.

In the evenings she would have to prepare her classroom for next day. Yet like a lot of men, he wasn't all bad and there were times when she had some feeling for him. She was very sad to be told he was dead. She especially didn't like it that he had committed suicide. It worried her. Had he been back to the flat, and found out she'd had the locks changed to keep him out? She would never know. Yet she didn't see what else she could do. She just couldn't have it. If only another solution could have been found.

The other interesting thing about Signora Ugolini was that she knew of a case in Rome of a Catholic priest who was having an affair with a woman. Was it naive or not of Olive to be surprised? It seemed to mean that there was enough of it around for even Signora Ugolini to have come across it in her own personal life. This was in 1966.

Then Olive went to Naples. Middle-aged Italians can be every bit as boring as any other middle-aged men, and Olive found herself in a carriage which was full of them. They were talking about prices, and as the Italian word for 'terrible' is nearly the same as the English one, she could understand that all right. Then she got out onto the platform to buy herself a bar of chocolate. When she told them how much it was, they told her, 'It shouldn't be that expensive, he knows you're foreign, he thinks you can't understand the money.' But when a man got out to buy one, he was charged the same. Olive hadn't been fiddled. As the train was pulling out of the station they were still going on about it in Italian.

'Prices these days, terrible, terrible!'

'I don't know what the world is coming to.'

Olive thought it was worse than being with a lot of housewives.

In Naples she stayed on a farm. They had a dog there that was tied up twenty-four hours a day. It was never let off its lead, and it was kept in a field all on its own with only a kennel. Olive took him out for a walk, which might have been the only one he'd ever had in his life. It upset her dreadfully. She hadn't liked it much in other places she'd stayed where the stray cats were as common as flies, but nothing was as bad as this dog. In fact the cats had once been quite amusing. She used to give them food, and they soon learned to come when they were called. One day she was calling, 'Puss, puss, puss!' and a man sitting on the balcony asked his wife what it meant. She told him, 'Puss is the English for cat.' At that moment three of the cats jumped over the wall. Everyone laughed. 'Look at that, you can't understand English but the cats can,' they said to him.

While in Naples she went as an interpreter to see a doctor with an English girl. She was horrified at what they were talking about, although she wasn't taken completely by surprise. It was a lady doctor, and she was laying down the terms for an abortion. Totally illegal in Italy. Anyway it turned out the girl wasn't pregnant. The doctor asked her, 'Who told you about me?'

The girl gave the name of another doctor in Naples. 'They're going to be found out' thought Olive.

Naples was a real dump and Olive was ill with diarrhoea while there, but then they say, 'See Naples and then die'. The poverty was dreadful. There would be children sleeping rough with their mothers. She heard an American woman saying, 'It makes me sick'.

The boat trips across to the islands around Naples were lovely, but nothing like as nice as the islands themselves. Especially Capri. The water was so clear and clean, and that was only the beginning of it. Yet again it went unsaid that the lady of the house never did any work, and yet again she was driven mad by the belief that it's the cold that causes a cold, or wearing no shoes. That was despite the fact the place was full of tourists, Americans, all with no shoes on, and none of them with a cold, yet the Italians continued to have their beliefs.

Olive wondered if maybe there was a grain of sense in it. It's true your resistance is more likely to be down. If the virus happens to be about, and if you have a lot of other things as well, like being badly nourished, then you are less likely to resist it. But why not say in that case you are likely to get chicken pox? Because it's the cold virus that is most likely to be around.

Samuel Pepys wrote in his diary that he had caught a cold from washing his feet. Olive heard another case where wearing a vest was considered very important and when a girl didn't, and got a cold the next day, it was put down to this.

It took Olive quite some while to tell a family that she believed it was all a lot of nonsense, and of course she didn't say it in a family where the children were small, or they would have thought she was unfit to look after them. With a slight smile, the Signora said to her, 'How can you say such things when so much research has been done on it, and there is so much evidence to prove that you are wrong?'

Olive said 'What research? You might find an individual doctor to back you up but you won't find any authority, it's a complete myth.'

Then they talked about a cure, and Olive told them about a lady doctor who said a cold treated lasted a fourteen days and a cold untreated lasted two weeks. The daughter, thinking it was Olive's Italian that was wrong, started explaining that this didn't make sense as the two times were the same. The mother understood it at once and said, 'Mary, they know that, they're taking the mickey.'

There was another example of it going unsaid that the wife never did any work. When working out a timetable, there was no suggestion that his wife should do any of it. It reminded her of the first family she had stayed with. An argument had broken out as to who should do some ironing. It was a living-in couple, and they were servants. The manservant said his wife already had far too much to do and Olive couldn't have agreed more, but it was early days for Olive in Italy. In all innocence she said, 'Maria is to tell Signora that she's not going to do it, then she'll come and ask me and I'll tell her I'm not going to do it, and then she will have to do it herself.' He refused to take this seriously, nor did he think that Olive was being serious. He thought she was being nasty.

She had one experience of a mother being just stupid. This woman would make a fuss about something like the toast being burnt, say she couldn't go away because Olive had shown how incapable she was, and then when something happened that really did matter you couldn't get her interested.

She had two boys, and Olive would go swimming with them in the sea. But they were going much too far out. They were also getting onto rocks and diving in. They could hit their heads on them and do quite a bit of injury; they might even knock themselves unconscious and be drowned. She told them to stop it, but they refused. They went on doing it, nor would they come nearer to the beach when she told them to. When she told the mother she got no support whatsoever. This was the woman who would make all the commotion if some toast was burnt.

Next day it looked like there was going to be a repeat performance. Olive was honestly worried about her own safety. They were swimming so far out to sea that she could see herself not being able to keep it up and get back to the shore. She thought she might be drowned, and told the Signora. She was told it would be all right, they could go on their own.

So the two little boys, aged six and eight, went out for a swim while Olive and the Signora stayed on the beach. The Signora was quite happy to lie in the sun and sunbathe, but Olive got no rest at all. As the boys got further and further out to sea she kept waking up the Signora to tell her, until she finally woke her up to say, 'I can only see dots in the distance, I'm not certain at all it's the boys.'

'It'll be all right' she said. And with that she went on dozing.

A few days later Olive received a letter from England about a girl of eighteen who was having trouble with someone who appeared to be miles away on a different planet. In this case the person had power. It was the headmistress in her school. Her mother was very much on her daughter's side but was treading very carefully. The girl was hoping to go to university and they could see the silly woman mucking up a reference.

It happened like this. Rita was coming down the school stairs with her school friend Margery when Margery used the word 'damn'. The headmistress heard, came out of her office, got the wrong girl and marched Rita into her office. Rita had been brought up not to tell tales, so she just stood to attention as she was told off.

It worried her parents. They could see this headmistress talking about her on some important document as though she was some sort of a dreadful hothead, for example on a reference. Her father wrote to the school about it. He made it sound as though it was he who was the silly old woman, not the headmistress. He was crawling to her. He said, 'I do just want you to know, it wasn't Rita that said, 'Damn', but please don't tell Rita that I have written in, she would be so furious with me.'

The headmistress then immediately marched Rita back into the office, demanding to know the name of the girl who had said it, and told her how she knew it wasn't her because her father had written in.

'Thank goodness I'm not dependent on this silly woman here for references' thought Olive. She was shocked by what idiots some people were, and how sometimes they got into positions of power.

The Signora was always telling Olive how bad her Italian was. As Olive had sometimes had difficulty in getting people to understand her, she fully accepted this. After she came back to England, she did try to pass Italian GCSE, and was thrilled by what a good mark she got, especially in the conversation. For a long time afterwards she believed she had been lucky to get the right examiner. Only years later did she wonder if perhaps she was quite good at the language. After all, she'd lived in the country for two years and spoken it every day. She also wondered if some of the people saying she spoke it badly were jealous because they couldn't speak English. She was so glad she'd taken the exam and not let them put her off.

Yet all Italians weren't stupid, and you could talk some sense into most of them. It was just a case of too much time and money, and they were quite capable of learning. One trained nursery nurse, very soon, very politely, told a mother that to keep on giving them opening medicine, in the long term, could cause cancer of the bowel.

'But he's always constipated' said the mother.

'He will be, the bowel gets lazy and dependent on it.'

The woman asked her doctor and after that she carefully weaned him off it.

Another trained nursery nurse was very fed up with it all. 'They don't know children' she said. It was ironic. Rightly so, the women would check up with references before having them, to see if the girl knew about children, but that would only be because it was routine. They didn't know how important it actually was. But the girls would want to know that about them. Did they know children? They would expect them to do things, blame them for things for which the children were doing, and they didn't know, that's children for you, a child will do that.

It's very easy to get common sense mixed up with common knowledge. And something may be only common knowledge in your circles or something you're trained in.

When talking about how dreadful some of these families could be, we need to hear both sides of the story. Here's one. Olive would go into the kitchen to talk to the servant girl after a dinner party and have a good tuck-in with her. There would also be a friend of the servant girl there who had also dropped in for a tuck-in. The family never objected to this. Then one day the husband put his head round the door and said to Olive, 'Come out of here.' He told the friend of the servant girl to go home. He then said to Olive that he'd had the girl's mother after him, saying he was working her daughter until eleven o'clock at night. She was only seventeen. Although this was true, she had been washing up until that time, there was no mention of what time the washing up was started. However there was no problem there. The girl's mother was perfectly willing to believe him.

It made Olive think about what is acceptable. They treated the servants so badly, yet there were days when slavery was fully accepted and you could even sell someone's daughter while they pleaded with you not to. Girls as young as thirteen were sold, and they never saw their mothers again. Are there people around today who would do that if they could? This man, who had daughters himself, lived in a world where parents had the rights over their teenage sons and daughters and nobody else, and most certainly not him. Yet he would do some things which Olive believed would never be accepted in England.

On the beach there was a photographer going up and down taking pictures of the children and then selling them to the parents. They were thrilled to have them. You couldn't do that today. No one was suspicious that he was up to something, and nor was he, but these days it would be asked if he was a paedophile.

Just before Olive returned to England, she saw a letter in the newspaper written by a young Italian girl, saying how impossible it was to go out and how they would harass her. She described what had happened when she had been trying to cross the road in Rome even during the day. Olive wondered if they were beginning to realise it wasn't acceptable.

She had the most dreadful time on her journey home. It was a journey through hell. It would have cost her much more to go by plane, yet she realised if ever she went again she'd have to. At one point she was driven into the corridor by a man, and even thought for a few seconds he might throw her off the train. She screamed, but he would not take no for an answer. As the train approached France, it got better, and she found that Frenchmen will leave you alone just as Englishmen usually do.

When she arrived in Dover it was glorious. A young Englishman got on the boat, with other porters, and said to her, 'Do you want any help with your baggage Madam?'

Calling her Madam was so respectful. It meant to her, 'I'm not going to start making advances to you.' The behaviour of so many Italian men was so disrespectful, sometimes alarming and in a train corridor, terrifying.

They would say the woman should take their advances as a compliment. They were flattering themselves.

CHAPTER 4

Olive continued to doze off as the coach drove away on its way to London. She was there again, getting off the boat, and she drifted back into another dream. Nigel was running towards her with his arms outstretched, but just as she held her arms out wide to greet him, she woke up with a jolt. The coach had stopped in a traffic jam. Soon they would be arriving in London. She had to wake up right away and realise she had left the misogynist who hated her and had to do her best to start off a new life of her own.

She got a taxi straight to the hotel, a small one that belonged to her friend Gina. They weren't doing all that well but Gina offered her a room at the top of the house, to pay her national insurance stamp, to give her a bit of money, and she could have her food there. She would also have plenty of time off to have a look round for somewhere else.

She went out for a walk. The streets were deserted as it was New Year's Day. She looked through the windows of some of the big houses. People were just getting over the Christmas and New Year's celebrations. She wondered if she could get a job in one of them.

She started work in the hotel next day, and she loved it, running up and down the stairs with all the dishes and doing the washing up. She wasn't paid to think; she was paid to work.

She knew that all these stairs were good exercise for keeping calcium in the bones; they wouldn't break so easily when she was old. Her future and her health had become quite an issue with her. She was well aware that in time stress can contribute to making someone very ill. In fact it was something she had tried to get James to take seriously. Once when she'd been away she'd posted something to him about it. He showed it her and said, 'This is from you isn't it?' Then he made certain she saw him rip it up and throw it in the bin. At the time she thought he just didn't accept it how ill he could make her. She didn't realise he knew all right, he just didn't care. He might even want it. He saw her as a fearful figure, a helpless victim, and if she was ill it would make her powerless.

There was always something going on in the hotel. Gina would tell her about it. She was just fed up with it all. One girl they'd sacked was going to an industrial tribunal for unfair dismissal, but Gina was determined not to have to pay her anything. This girl had been booking people in at night and if they left early the next morning before anyone got up and saw, she wouldn't register them – she would pocket the money for herself.

They had no end of trouble with people pinching things. A large picture was taken off a wall during a wedding reception. The staff said someone must surely have seen it go. It was very mysterious. They never found out who had taken it.

Then they saw someone take an expensive vase and hide it under his mackintosh. The staff blocked all exits and never took their eyes off him for a second. When he went to tell them he couldn't get out, they told him why. They said, 'The police are on their way and we know where you've got a vase hidden.' When they arrived they arrested him.

The job didn't last. Firstly Olive couldn't manage on such a small amount of money. Secondly staff kept changing, with a lot of part-timers coming and going, and some of them would be niggling over the least little thing. There was a really quarrelsome atmosphere. She couldn't stand it. It was what she'd come to get away from.

Yet she felt sad on her last day, and before she went she had a good natter with the girl in the next room, Gillian. Somehow, if you know you're not going to see someone again, you don't mind opening your heart to them.

They sat by the window looking down on the busy road below; it was beginning to go dark and people were bustling from one place to another. A tramp was about to settle down for the night, in a back doorway. Gillian had also had trouble with misogyny. She had helped pay towards her boyfriend's car and then, as soon as he got the money, he turned nasty. During a phone call he'd taken offence at something she'd said, saying that she was accusing him of spying on her. He wouldn't let her speak, ranting on and finishing up with, 'Go and find some other spy'.

He put the phone down on her. Gillian knew it wasn't really a row, that he was just acting, yet it still very much alarmed her. She had met such dreadful men before, but she didn't know there was a name for them.

He turned up later at the hotel as though nothing had happened. He was planning a drama, a pretty scene in which they could have a pretty reconciliation. She said to him, 'Go away, go away!' but he then turned nasty in a way she had never seen him before. He looked like a real lout and before that he had always seemed quite a gentleman. It frightened her very much. He was calling her 'Your sort' and she wondered what he meant by that and what 'sort' he thought she was. But he did go. Maybe because she knew things about him which were confidential.

No one could think what he meant by 'your sort'. She asked several people. It puzzled her for days. But then none of them knew about misogyny, as this was still the 1980s. Would they know now? She was the sort of woman he feared. He saw that in her.

Then Gillian went back to her teenage years. She had a party in her house one night, and her mother had taken a particular dislike to one of the young men there. Jim. She said he was either stupid or nasty and whichever it was she couldn't cope with it. Gillian couldn't see that he was bad at all, but then she hadn't been there at the time of the incident. Apparently he was supposed to be going out with a girl called Janet who got to the party a little before him, and he turned up with a girl called Rose. Gillian just thought that Janet had jumped to conclusions and made claims upon him too soon. Now she wondered. Perhaps he hated women. Now she knew it was a symptom of misogyny to try to get a row going between two women.

Gillian's mother was such a nice lady; it wasn't like her to take an immediate dislike to someone. What did she smell? She'd had no tuition in misogyny. Gillian and Olive talked about it until the early hours of the morning, as the rush in the street below got quieter; the tramp in the doorway had now gone and the road sweepers were busy at work. They found they were beginning to hate men as they talked on. It's catching. The bit Gillian really did remember was when she told her mother that this man, Jim, was in a sanatorium for tuberculosis. She gave out a sigh as though she was disgusted, and then slowly said, 'Well I suppose I should be sympathetic, but I just think ugh, on top of everything else about him he's got tuberculosis.'

Olive remembered as a teenager going to a dance. A good-looking man called Arnold was going to take her home. She was thrilled. Then she discovered he was supposed to be the boyfriend of a close friend of hers, Doreen. She thought they'd broken up. She and Doreen nearly fell out over it. Now, so many years later, she felt certain he had done it on purpose to cause trouble between the two women. He had failed. Fortunately they both had good parents who they could talk to about it. In fact one of them had just given up working nights, saying that this was the time when her teenage daughter would need her and there she was at the right time with her husband, the girl's father. Yet they should both have known something about misogyny.

She didn't have any more to do with him, but later on she heard about something else very odd which he did when messing about with a woman, Anna. He kept giving her various people's phone numbers, telling her he would be there at a certain time and could she please phone him. When she did so no one knew where he was. After three times she stopped. When later someone told her that Arnold had been complaining she'd been making a nuisance of herself, kept phoning him up at other peoples' houses, in all innocence she said, 'No he wouldn't have said that, that'll be someone else he's talking about, he keeps asking me to phone him'.

'I know' she was told. 'Nevertheless he's been saying you are making a nuisance of yourself.'

She was astonished. She asked then how did people think she'd managed to get hold of their number, to be quickly assured that this had been noticed and commented upon. The discussion had been on what a peculiar thing for him to do and not about her.

Another time this Doreen had come in late at night, thoroughly fed up about a man. He had been one of a crowd, and his language had been appalling. In those days men just didn't swear in front of women, or at least not unless they knew that woman extremely well. It's a good warning signal for a woman. Yet they didn't know it's also a symptom of misogyny to want to insult, and that this man had found a good way to insult a woman.

Doreen and her parents then got onto the subject of the 1930s and what went on when they were young. There were plenty of bad language and dirty jokes in those days all right between members of the opposite sex, but only when they knew each other very well, the same as it would be these days. They gave Anneliese as an example. She was 19, a German Jew who had escaped the camps. She later married a British Jew. She met him at Reading University, and being students at the same time both her parents knew them extremely well. Doreen's mother said, 'Anneliese wouldn't have minded telling your father a dirty joke.'

Anneliese had indeed been a victim of hate, but her brother far more so, for although she had escaped the camps her 21-year-old brother hadn't been so lucky. On a cold bitter night in Germany, the police had arrived for him and taken him away. They never saw him again. They took all his clothes off and put him out in the station yard. He didn't last the night. They then went to tell his mother what had happened and asked her what they should do with his clothes.

They had been up to the house before. They had taken the wedding ring off the mother's finger, a gold one, and said, 'You know we don't steal, we never steal', and they gave her a penny for this ring.

Whatever is it that makes people so sick, hate someone so much, because of the colour of their skin or because of what sex they are? Maybe they just hate humanity and will use anything as an excuse

Olive felt sad that she would be leaving the hotel later that morning. Then Freda came into the room to join them. She'd just got up and still had her dressing gown on. It was five o'clock. When she joined in the conversation and said how she hated men, Olive realised there must be some connection. It wasn't so much that the owner, Gina, was sympathetic with this sort of thing; it was that she knew something about it. She recognized the symptoms and her name was getting about. Consequently the hotel started getting full of them.

Freda's husband couldn't manage money. As soon as he had any he spent it. She had always tried to tell him that it's not so much how much you've got coming in but how much you've got going out. He was extremely bitter that she was so 'rich.' He was like a child who knows what a lot of money the daily help has because he's seen her purse. Yet it was very frightening the way he wouldn't keep quiet about her 'riches'. She first began to realise this when she had a picture delivered at her house. He was greatly exaggerating its value, and going round all the bookies and rough pubs talking about it. She feared she would have her house broken into. As he was away a lot she feared this would be when she was on her own. Who might she find in her room when she woke up in the middle of the night? It didn't cross her mind that maybe he'd arrange it.

It was dreadful some of the people he'd mix with. Yet there was one man who lived down the road who didn't seem too bad, although he was an alcoholic and was nicknamed Alky. One night she'd had a very big row with her husband and after it they all went out for a drink. Alky told her two things. Firstly, he realised how much he'd been lied to. Her husband had raged about her as though she was absolutely dreadful. In fact, asking her to excuse the expression, he said he had believed that she was just some horrible old witch. He admitted to it, he had just been completely taken in.

The other thing he told her was far more horrific. Freda had just sold one house and was about to buy another. In the middle of moving, she had been in possession of a cheque for £32,000. Now that's a lot of money if it's pocket money, if it can be spent on a night out, but it can seem very little if you've got to buy another house with it. He would never take into consideration things like having a mortgage to pay off. She was very frightened.

About a week later Alky was murdered. He had bought some stolen goods from the person who had stolen them from the burglars, and the original burglars came back for them. They knocked him about quite a bit before killing him. He was found next day behind a door with a knife through his heart. They got the two men the following day.

When people first heard Alky was dead they thought it was suicide. He had been in a depressed condition because his mother had recently died. In fact, he had talked of killing himself and someone else had been inside the house and removed all the knives. They thought it wouldn't have happened if his mother had been alive. His father was aware that some sort of a fight was starting up but in that house there always was. Yet if his 'fusspot' mother had been there she'd have called the police. She was always getting them in.

But back to the bit that concerns Freda. She thought it would be an ideal opportunity to try to get her husband to understand he was not to talk about money. She said, 'I hope those men don't think I've got a lot. I hope they don't think I've got £32,000 and they're telling the other jailbirds this when they're about to come out.'

It wasn't until some years later that she realised what a complete waste of time it was. She received a phone call from a woman called Laura, someone else who was permanently drunk, and clearly she had been told how very wealthy Freda was.

Freda then telephoned another friend of his and was lucky enough to get him sober, which most certainly made a change. In fact it changed him completely; it was as though he had climbed out of his grave and was back to his old self. He was sensible and sympathetic. He spoke to her slowly, as though to break it to her gently, that he was afraid that rumour had it that her husband was married to a very rich woman. It reminded Olive of another case where a man had been in a chip shop talking about an elderly lady who had a lot of money.

Drug addicts, anyone, could have heard this, and when the old lady heard about it she had to make certain her house was very well locked up. In that case too, it would have been a waste of time telling this man he was greatly endangering her. He wouldn't be able to understand that and it might even make him shout it out more. He too had some of the symptoms of misogyny. Do these men want women to be robbed and beaten up?

If only she could have stayed in the hotel with them for a bit longer, but it was very near time for leaving. She had to go. Fortunately one of the guests at the hotel, a Madame Paree, had heard her talking and offered her somewhere to stay. It was in the basement of a tall house; you could almost call it a cellar. It had been completely separate, but she and her husband had re-opened the door at the top of the stairs.

'I'm not as lazy as that.' Olive laughed when she first saw them doing it, but later she found out there was another reason. If she didn't live completely separately then this would make the law more favourable for the landlord. In fact they would never have offered it to her in the first place but for this. It was lucky they had heard her saying she wanted somewhere where the landlady could sometimes cook for her. She was going to go up there for some of her meals.

The basement and the rest of the rooms in the house had been empty for years; in fact, ever since the law had come in on the side of the tenant, making it harder to get them out. Solicitors were very strongly advising their clients not to let.

It created quite a problem, as without the rent they could no longer get the repairs done and the house was slowly deteriorating and getting damp, yet the solicitor would continue telling them not to let. 'Don't come to me in a few years' time and tell me you can't get these people out,' he would say.

It had become known as 'Jacksonism' in their street, meaning bad and scrounging tenants, forcing landlords with a lot less money than they had to give them large sums of money to leave. There were other ways they could bully them. The landlord might be afraid to do anything in case they called it harassment and got the police in. There were some very sad stories about this.

In fact the word 'Jacksonism' came from a Mrs Jackson, a case that had been highlighted in the papers. She had occupied most of the house, and the landlady downstairs had only two rooms and desperately needed the rest of the house back again. Her daughter was expecting a baby and they were all squashed up together. None of them had anything like as much money as Mrs Jackson. They weren't allowed to put her rent up; she paid very little, yet they were expected to do repairs. It meant the landlady had to go out to work to keep her own tenant. Mrs Jackson didn't have to work as she had such a lot of money. She also had a car, although she didn't need one. The landlady could well have done with one, for example to get to work instead of having to hang around windy bus stops, but she couldn't even afford driving lessons.

When she lost a court case to get possession she nevertheless evicted Mrs Jackson, so she went to prison for contempt of court. When she came out she immediately evicted her again, so she went to prison again.

Then Mrs Jackson left. No one knew why; it was very sudden, though it's believed she couldn't stand all the bad publicity. Some of the louts who read about it harassed her, which wasn't to help the poor landlady; some people will do anything in the name of caring.

Olive managed to get a job in a shop selling clothes. Business wasn't good and she knew she had to sell, as otherwise the money for her wages wouldn't be there. She would have to tell the customers they looked nice in anything they tried on, regardless of whether or not they did. It was shop policy and the manageress told her to do it.

They had a row of labels under the counter and if they didn't have the size the customer asked for they would switch them round. Sometimes though the customer would be too vain to admit to their size. Even if they did have it, they would still switch it round to the size they were asked for.

Olive settled into the basement, feeling very safely tucked away. Would she ever go back to her husband? People could call her a fool for marrying him in the first place, but they should be fully in the picture first. The Mental Health Act 1983 was wide open to abuse. It wasn't safe for Olive to be single. She had a bully of a sister, and it was thoroughly dangerous that she was being forced to accept her as her nearest relative. It might allow the sister to get a lot of power.

Medical opinions don't have to be based on facts - beliefs will do. If a complaint has been put in about someone they can act upon it without investigating it. There's nothing in the Mental Health Act to say they've got to look into it. They've no need to try. They can even refuse. A person can be guilty until proved innocent. In this case there wasn't even any need for there to be a social worker in the first place. She was only involved because she was going by what some idiot had told her. A person can be sectioned up to 28 days before seeing a tribunal, before being able to insist that any opinion they are acting upon is based on facts that are correct. A lot of damage can be done in that time.

The most serious thing of all was that the sister was making the claim that she cared about her; 'My interest is to help' she said. The Mental Health Act is especially open to abuse if this claim is being made and especially if they have a social worker to say she believes it, even more if the social worker is making this claim too, as was the case here. The sister could tell the social worker anything about Olive, and just as long as it was something bad she would act upon it. A solicitor told Olive she was not to let them inside the house, for although they would give Olive a chance to tell her side of the story, whatever they said could be used as evidence against her. They could refuse to believe it, without looking into it, and say it was delusional and take her sister's word for everything. But now she was married, her sister was no longer her nearest relative. She had lost all her power.

Olive began to wonder how much of the story that she had bullied her little sister a lot as a child was because her parents had kept family deaths a secret from her, and how much because she was being bullied so much by her big sister. She had always made it clear to her that she was inferior, a fool, and embarrassing to be with.

Misogyny reminded Olive of what she had read about mental hospitals, only in malpractice of course, the exceptions, and although this is rare it isn't that rare. They don't want the patient to get better; they want control. The women can be as bad as the men; in fact it can sometimes be the women rather than the men who are doing it. It can happen where the staff and a patient swap roles; the patient is being most tactful, while the member of staff is doing their best to stir things up and to get things going. People say the same thing about the police.

A lot of people believe that rape is a sex crime, but it's far more than that, it's a crime of power. Some men rape their wives. Other women have been raped who would have consented had they been properly approached. Some of the power freaks who have worked in mental hospitals could very easily have got them to volunteer, but they don't want that. The patient has to be forced and subjugated.

One night Olive had a dream. She dreamed that a burglar got inside her house, and he was upstairs and she was downstairs; she knew this not only because she could hear him walking about but because quite clearly someone had climbed in through the kitchen window. In fact, that would be virtually impossible for anyone to do as the window had been so securely put in, but it happened in the dream. She knew this was telling her nothing is safe. Olive had believed she was well protected, that the Mental Health Act was as safe as her kitchen window, and that they had to try to investigate any allegations made against someone if they were going to act upon them. But the Act was as open to abuse as her kitchen window. In fact, in her dream there was no window there at all; the burglars had taken it away and there was just a hole in the wall.

Then in her dream a friend appeared. He put his arm round her and said, 'The burglar is still upstairs and he hasn't found any of your valuables, I am keeping them safe for you'. Olive knew this was telling her that despite the Mental Health Act being so very dangerous, there are still people around who will keep you safe. She knew, for example, the solicitor who told her she was not to let them into the house.

CHAPTER 5

Olive, Freda and Gillian had agreed to meet again. One of them knew of a women's group and they decided to go there. Olive went once, but never again. It was run by Women's Lib activists and they were more than fanatical, they hated men. Yet she had to admit, they say it's the fanatics that get something done, and there were no other campaigns that had done so much for her.

Olive also wondered if fighting for equality of the sexes can turn into hate because the root of the problem wasn't first looked into. Were the women who were fighting for equality in the sixties victims of misogyny? Yet if she went back further she had to exclude Emily Pankhurst, the one who got the women the vote. From what she'd read she had a very good father and although he wasn't particularly into women's rights he did other things, like campaigning to abolish slavery.

There was a case of a woman who was told she couldn't have a washing machine unless her husband signed for it. A few years ago Olive would never had let anything like that bother her but now she too would never tolerate it.

At this meeting there was a man in the room who was not allowed to speak. Every time he tried to, he was immediately shouted down, and sometimes a woman would point a finger straight at him. It was blatantly obvious that this was because he was a man. They were either discriminating or generalizing about the lot of them.

They then went onto discuss other things, until it came to talking about some women using vaginal creams and how to stop them. Olive said they were causing irritation and husbands had been told to stop their wives using them. Their faces lit up then and they started laughing. Clearly they enjoyed the thought of it. It disgusted Olive. But she thought they were joking when they said, 'We'll leave that one out then.'

She also found it distasteful enjoying the thought of a man itching in his privates. Olive wanted to say to them, 'What's the matter with you?'

There was one nice woman at the meeting; her name was Jo-Ann. Some years ago she had had some dreadful trouble with a man called Bruce. He thought she hadn't got the right to leave him and he had sought horrific revenge. What next? Perhaps he'd strangle her. It was also typical of some of these cases where there is plenty of dirty washing being hung up in public. She had to get out of where she was living and hope he wouldn't find her. In desperation she asked the help of her ex-boyfriend's mother and got it, but it was all very awkward as the boyfriend was now married to someone else. His mother, Mrs Swann, gave up her front room for her and made it into a bedroom. Jo-Ann kept making promises she would find somewhere else as quickly as she could and in fact, in time, she did find other lodgings. She had lost her flat through it as her boyfriend, Bruce, had got in and wrecked the place. She shared it with two other girls, one of whom owned it, and Jo-Ann didn't even ask, 'Do you mind if I come back?'

She was too embarrassed to show her face. It wasn't so much that they didn't want her, it was that they didn't dare with him around. Olive wondered if Mrs Swann could let her have a room all to herself, a bed sitter she could call her own, but she too, before considering it, was waiting to see if the law on eviction would change. Jo-Ann was another victim of the problem that nearly all the scrupulous landlords had now stopped letting, and if you managed to get a landlord at all, he might not care what the law was.

One problem Jo-Ann and others were hearing about was that although tenants were going to have no problem in proving it, and it was totally against the law what he was doing, the landlord didn't seem to be afraid of going to prison. He would be going down for other things in any case, nothing to do with letting, and any sentence he got for that would just run alongside the others.

Although there have always been some very bad landlords and their tenants needed protection, and indeed some were well protected, nevertheless it caused another big problem. Scrupulous landlords weren't going to risk letting. If it meant they couldn't get rid of bad tenants, they closed the house down. When this was followed by a situation where only rogues were willing to let, it seemed to some people that this showed more than ever how these laws were needed to protect the tenants.

One young couple with two small children were very glad to have eventually found a house to live in. Then the landlord disappeared. Although this left them with all the repairs to see to, not a part of the contract, it did nevertheless mean they had no rent to pay. And that was a part of the contract. They wondered if it was even his house. Most certainly criminals were cashing in on the fact that people were desperate for somewhere to live. They would demand very high deposits. This young couple just did not know what the legal position would be if the original owners turned up. True they hadn't paid any rent for quite a few years, but they had also spent quite a few thousand on the house.

As regards men, both Olive and Jo-Ann came across something very much worse. It was when a Mrs Needham let a flat on top of a shop to a girl called Lulu. Lulu had had to flee her own country because she was a Christian, yet when in Britain she was under suspicion of not being one, and the authorities were suggesting she was making this up in order to get asylum. Mrs Needham was confident that this was not the case and said, 'Although you may succeed in telling a lie you won't succeed in living it'.

She didn't like their methods of finding out - they were seeing how well she knew her bible. Mrs Needham had found that the two things didn't necessarily go together. In fact, she had known people who were well read up on Christianity in order to oppose it. She also knew of a case of someone who knew her bible very well, and it wasn't because she was a Christian but a vegetarian who had been to a church feast. She later pointed several things out to them, for example in Leviticus where it told you not to eat blood. How can you eat meat and not blood? Impossible. Yet this vegetarian hadn't meant to show them bits which she knew about and they didn't. She didn't want to embarrass them, in fact she wished she'd got them more prepared for it. Her only interest had been to let them see that there was plenty in the bible in favour of not eating meat.

Yet Lulu, this Christian refugee, didn't feel safe in Britain for other reasons too. Would she ever feel safe again? Even in Britain, Christians can be persecuted by people from their own country, and even by members of their own family.

Lulu, the first refugee to arrive at the flat, didn't seem to know any other life than living dangerously. She and another girl who later arrived, called Mo, had stories to tell which the British would find unbelievable. Mo had escaped first from the Middle East to Australia and a Muslim man there noticed that she was reading the bible. He told her that anyone who killed her for this crime would go to heaven. Then he lured her to a farm, telling her that her friends were there. They weren't of course. She managed to escape, eventually finishing up in London, but she felt she had had a narrow escape.

Neither Olive nor Mrs Needham had any understanding of this. They were both Christians, yet it did seem to them that some people use religion in order not just to get power but to put it to bad use. They most certainly knew at the same time that a lot of very good work went on in the church, although it did have an appalling history.

But what Olive found most disturbing was this. One refugee they were told about was on the run from his father because he had said he would kill him. He was told that no father would do that to his own son. Is this ignorance or denial? Whichever it is, it's thoroughly dangerous if a man can be refused asylum on those grounds, as some of these families are dreadful.

Neither Lulu nor Mo stayed very long at Mrs Needham's. Instead they found a living-in job for a very rich family; it suited them fine, as they wanted to be together. Mrs Needham then took in another girl, an English one this time, thinking there would be no more trouble like before, only to find there was nothing but trouble, all the time. Sometimes it would involve Mrs Needham, although she was not a resident landlady. The girl seemed to want to be dominated, to be beaten up. She had a man friend who would do this to her time and time again, and she would go back to him time and time again. She would have one excuse after another for doing so and didn't seem to realise how much it was affecting everyone else. She once telephoned Social Services from a call box on Christmas Day saying that he had gone off and taken all her clothes with him and she had nothing on. They sent someone out to see to it.

It made Olive point something out to Jo Ann. Since then, thirteen years before when she had had all this trouble, she had never had another man friend. Now she was 35. 'Were you put off men for life?' she asked her. She didn't know, she had never really thought about it, but she had certainly lost all interest in them after that.

The work in the shop started going badly for Olive. A supermarket opened up nearby, so that was her out of a job. They weren't selling things and then there was a big row about a coat that was pinched. Someone from high up came to interview them all about it. Poor old Betty, who had only come down for the day from another department, got it in the neck. Someone had asked for something that was in the window and she'd gone out with them to see it. She was told that with all her experience she should have sent someone else out. Meanwhile the coat had gone.

One of the girls told her that stealing had completely ruined one Christmas for her. She had been working in a very small shop and they had decided to order four coats, very good ones. They took a risk there because if they didn't sell them they would lose a lot of money. One of them was stolen. During this girl's Christmas holidays she and her family discussed whether she should try to find some other kind of work, as the stealing was so upsetting.

Olive decided to leave - they didn't need her any more. She'd go back to her husband. Perhaps he'd be better now that she'd been gone over a year.

It was lovely to be on the train and not to have to go to work. She sat there relaxing, waiting for the train to leave, slowly drinking a cup of hot coffee as she watched everyone else rushing about, making certain they got to work on time. How lovely it was that she didn't have to.

As the train drew out of the station the guard at one end shouted to the driver at the other end, 'What's up with you?' The driver shouted back at him, 'No, what's up with you? This train should have been out a long time ago.' Then a member of staff standing on the station shouted, 'No consideration.'

The passengers all sat there grinning. Clearly they were enjoying it. Anything which takes away dignity is fun. It's almost as though having to wait some time for a train to go out is worth it. Besides, Olive and some of the other passengers had thought it was the next train going out too early - they hadn't realised it was the one before going out late.

She began to think deeply as the train chugged along. How far would some people go if given a chance? She remembered a case she'd read about in Scotland, many years ago. An old woman who lived in the Highlands with her family was very unattractive with her various ailments, with a very arthritic hand. They feared she would be called a witch. The family agreed that her cat had to go. In any case it wasn't safe for the cat. They would burn that along with her. They kept her hidden away in the back room as much as they could. That wasn't difficult. She was old and frail, she didn't want to go out much and she stayed quite cheerful. They wondered how aware she was of what was going on. Psychiatrists reckon it was men who hated women who were behind it, burning women as witches.

As the train continued to chug along she wished so much she could get two amendments put into the Mental Health Act 1983. One was, if the nearest relative used their powers unreasonably, the patient should be able to get them removed. The other was, that the Mental Health Team can only act upon facts that are correct. She felt it would change her life if she could get those two changes made. Her husband was nothing like as bad as her sister. He wasn't evil. He wasn't making up information and phoning up Social Services with it.

She thought about James. He was bad, but nothing like as bad as that. When they'd got married, as soon as they came out of the registrar's office she'd whispered in his ear, 'I really mean every promise I've made.'

But he wanted someone to hate. He wanted someone he could have a stormy relationship with. Olive found that out very soon indeed. Within three weeks, she was asking a solicitor if she could get a divorce on grounds of cruelty. Yet before she had married him she had studied this subject carefully. She knew he'd had a difficult relationship with another woman. She was well aware some men enjoy the conflict. She wondered if behind all his complaining about it, he was loving it really and was it him who was stirring it all up? But after getting to know him for five months and being with him night and day, she felt certain it wasn't. She felt he just wanted to settle down for a quiet life.

But she was wrong. He didn't. He wanted another woman to have another stormy relationship with and he wanted one in which he could force her to do what she didn't want to do. For example, he didn't want her to do any of the cooking or housework as this was something she loved doing so much.

He refused to eat with her. She felt that eating together was as important as sleeping together and that the marriage hadn't been consummated. Every day he would tell her, 'Today will be your day.' He would promise her he would be in for dinner. She would get it all ready for him and then he wouldn't turn up. If he did come back he would look at it and say, 'Sorry, I can't face that.' She wondered how he could be so cruel.

One night when he came in and he said this, another man in the house said he'd have it instead. He felt sorry for her. Then James said he was just popping out for something. After he returned he sat between the two of them having supper together. He pretended he was hiding something, but he wanted her to see it all right. He was nibbling away at a bar of chocolate. He wanted to insult her. He hated her.

Sometimes when they went out in the morning he would tell her he had no appetite for breakfast. But as soon as they got out he would say he was hungry and tell her, 'That looks like a nice coffee bar, let's go and see if we can get something to eat'. He would really wind her up; get her to throw crockery at him, in her desperation and in a plea to get him to be nice to her. At that stage she was completely confused about it all. Yet you couldn't call it a row, not if one side was busy enjoying it even if the other was deeply upset. He would create a situation in which he would look very much he was in the right. Maybe you could say the woman was in the wrong and she wasn't to give him a reaction. How easy it is to tell her she's not to lose her calm, if it's not that person who's got it to put up with. It can then all sound like common sense.

Yet Olive found it impossible, as he would do one thing after another knowing full well how much it would be upsetting her. Nor would it be true to say, if she gave him a reaction he would do it more. He would do it in any case, or find some other way to wind her up. It's not to be compared with things like kids playing knock and run. It's something far deeper than that.

James seemed to want to show everyone what an impossible wife he had. He would show people the mess after crockery had been thrown about. He had no interest in her health. Her neck was so stiff there had to be something seriously wrong with it. Olive thought maybe a big piece of fat had jammed inside it. It felt like it. She didn't realise it was probably all due to the great stress she was under.

She did two things which were probably cries for help. She had hoped he would show some compassion when he saw the pitiful state she was in. She had an appointment to see her doctor in the morning and when she found it difficult to get dressed, she went there in a taxi in her dressing gown. Another time she called out a doctor in the middle of the night. It was all in vain. James had no interest in her whatsoever. He even threatened her once to throw her downstairs as she struggled with her neck.

There can be a big problem with getting help if you have a stress-related illness, or at least if it would be a good thing for you to have some counselling. A lot of these charities won't do it unless you tell them who your doctor is; they will just close the door in your face if you refuse to, maybe because they are government funded and they have to sign contracts in order to get any money. They did dare not to believe anything other than it was a matter of the patient's safety to know this, and many of them would even couple the word 'safe' with the word 'doctor' as though they were the same thing. It definitely came under mental health. They would talk to her as though she might be a danger to herself, and at times even a threat to someone else, and until she realised it was the money that was the problem she found she had no faith in them if they had so much faith in doctors. Olive already knew that when the government gave the Mental Health Team a lot of power with their opinions that they had left it very open to abuse. She thought it was because they were in denial, and it came to no surprise to her that this was followed by all this red tape.

There was another thing: a counsellor might have a hang up about something or do something very silly, completely misinterpreting what a client had said and saying something dangerous to the doctor about it. Yet despite all this Olive knew that as a rule most doctors were efficient and dedicated in their work; it was merely that there were enough exceptions around for it to matter. Most certainly it was for her alone to decide which risk to take and when she would see a doctor. She could always see her own, there was no risk there.

One day she was lying on the couch and found that the effort to lift her head and the strain it put on her neck was terrific. She would try to take the weight off by lifting her head with her hands. She asked James if he could make her a cup of coffee and he did do, but it was almost cold. Very timidly she asked him, 'Can't I have nice hot cup?' and he started shouting aggressively at her.

Another time she was in bed when he started climbing onto it. 'Can't you go upstairs?' she pleaded. 'My neck's so bad and the least little movement is agony.' He told her it was his bed, he would sleep wherever he liked, and he made a point of bouncing about heavily when getting into it.

At Christmas time she had toothache and all the dentists were closed. She was trying so hard to nurse her bad tooth, but it was impossible; as she lay there he was doing one thing after another to wind her up. She had to jump up several times. She said to him, 'It's unbelievable.' There was no feeling whatsoever for her. When does it reach a stage when it's more than cruel - it's wicked?

With the telephone he found he could really manipulate her. She would have a dreadful time because he would refuse to speak to her on it. By now they were only semi-living together. She could still go and stay with friends. But she was always afraid to say anything to him on the phone in case he put it down on her. It was making her a nervous wreck. It got so that if she spoke to anyone at all on the phone, she would start to fear they were going to do the same thing. She would have to remind herself that they wouldn't, they were not like him.

Sometimes, as soon as he heard her voice he would put the phone down. Sometimes he would just put it on the table, and she wouldn't realise he wasn't listening. He would especially do this if there were other people in the room. In fact, it would only be when she'd hear him talking to someone else that she realised he'd done it. He liked to have an audience.

Yet she should have seen the writing on the wall. He used to do that to his mother. He also used to talk viciously about her, but it wasn't until later Olive discovered there might be some connection. It could be that fear and need for her had started off his fear of women.

In fact, when he started doing it to Olive with an audience, the same thing happened as had with his mother. The audience were most embarrassed. Olive had rushed to tell his mother she wasn't a party to it; then later people rushed to tell Olive that they weren't a party to what James did.

There was no persuading him. It could mean she would have to walk through the town late at night, among the drunks, very frightened. He cared no more for her safety than he did for her health.

One day she arrived with a bad chest, and she was especially out of breath as she'd had to climb a steep hill. When she got home, she found the receiver off the hook. She knew it would be as when she had tried to call him earlier she had continually got the engaged signal. She sat down on the floor against some cushions facing him. He started lighting up a cigarette.

'Oh please don't smoke!' she cried out, 'My chest is so bad, I can hardly breathe.' But he continued to do so and then puffed smoke straight into her face.

The trouble was, when anyone phoned him and got no reply, they never knew if he had taken the wire out of the wall or if he wasn't there. They would have to go over to see. This was especially awkward for Olive if their dog needed seeing to. Olive had managed to get someone to help her with it, much as she hated asking favours, and the man had a heart condition and was not to be exposed to stress. Olive carefully explained this to James.

'Oh please! Don't manipulate me by manipulating him,' she said. But it was all in vain. When this man could get no answer he had to go over, and when he got there, he found him there but the wire not in the wall.

It was with the phone that she concluded that she felt certain of it; it wasn't really a row on his part, and he was just enjoying it all. One day when she had to go round, very upset, she found him sitting with the receiver off the hook, watching television. Can you put a row on hold? No, you're too upset. That's not a row. That's an example of acting. She wondered how he could do that to her. She wouldn't be able to do that to anyone else. If someone was very upset, she couldn't just leave them there, she'd have to put things right before she started enjoying herself again.

They say that underneath it all a man is really a frightened little boy. Olive soon found this out, yet she didn't think it meant she should have it to put up with it. She also knew that if she tried to she would be risking her health.

There's no cure for it. Think of a man who has a broken back. He's a paraplegic for life. Although it's true he can't just be left and has to be given aids, like a wheelchair, he still shouldn't cause an obstruction and downright refuse to get out of the way.

James had had a tempestuous life. His parents had travelled abroad a lot and consequently he had gone to boarding school. It seems it wasn't a bad one; there was no bullying, as in so many. They taught him what he needed to know, although he didn't leave with brilliant marks. He found it jolly handy that he could speak French and later he spent a lot of time in France using that. He also did a lot of sport, and loved it; was always on the playing field, and this might account for him having very good blood pressure later in life. That was despite his heavy drinking, smoking and doing everything else they say you shouldn't. He seemed to hate the world and to defy everyone, the whole of the time.

He was also bad at managing money. As soon as he got any he

spent it, and then he would feel resentful, as though he had been done a dreadful injustice, and would sit and look very miserable and expect everyone else to be miserable too.

Olive tried to get housekeeping money from him when they were living together. He would make her work so hard for it that it wasn't worth it. He hadn't worked for years. When he went to get the dole, she would have to go with him, or he would spend it all before he got home. He would walk far too fast, making her having to chase after him, shouting, 'Wait for me, wait for me'.

At this stage she didn't realise how much he loved an audience. Once he started giving her a lot of notes out in the street. She tried hard to keep her voice down as she pleaded with him, 'Don't let people see you; I'm going to get robbed.'

But he made certain everyone saw. He shouted so aggressively at her, and gave it so openly to her, ten and twenty pound notes, that everyone turned round. She walked home looking over her shoulder the whole of the time, wondering who had seen.

He would buy a picture for hundreds of pounds and then when he ran out of money the next day he'd sell it for £10. This habit of spending his money as soon as he got it spoilt their holiday in Ostend. On the very first morning, he had drawn a picture, paid to have it framed and also bought another picture. They went home early after that, straight away. Olive couldn't enjoy a holiday with no money. They couldn't take either of the pictures with them as they had too much other baggage, so they left them in the hotel room.

It made her feel sick, people pleading poverty who were not poor. They wrecked it for people who really were. She had just been reading a book on the Poor Law of 1834. It was the same thing going on then. Some people would abuse it, which made it very difficult for people who genuinely needed to take or want to give. In 1834 they decided to make workhouses harder in order to stop scroungers getting in, and the same thing happened as does these days; power freaks started getting control. Their interest wasn't to keep the scroungers out. So what do we do about it? Should we let the needy starve because we can't manage it? You can't blame the authorities. It's the scroungers that are to blame.

Before she married James, he had been complaining bitterly about what he called 'hanger ons'. Indeed, his house had become notorious for it. It would be full of down and outs, alcoholics and the like.

In fact he had once been an alcoholic himself, but he was now dry and it was poison to him. He immediately gave it up after a perforated ulcer. He was very frightened by it. He'd been rolling all over the floor in absolute agony. If he hadn't been operated on within an hour he would have been dead.

Now that she knew he was not a helpless victim of these undesirable characters, that he was inviting them into the house, she started making certain that her own was well locked up when going away. The council had now found him a bed sitter. However things were going very wrong there, so he made her big promises that as it was her place, if she would let him stay there while she was away, he would make certain that only he was in the house.

And so with promises that he wouldn't invite anyone in she relented and let him have the key. It wasn't that as soon as her back was turned that he was inviting just anyone, it was as soon as he could slap her across the face with it. She realised this when she was talking to him on the phone. Very shocked that he had so immediately gone back on his word, she pleaded with him, 'I can't go back there to live! Not if you've got all these people in!'

He demanded that she should go straight back again. He said 'You can't expect me to be here all on my own.' At this stage she knew nothing about misogyny and did not realise that he only wanted her back to control her.

She phoned up a neighbour to ask him how many people were staying there. He said there were eight, but he did say not all of them were undesirable characters; some of them were quite pathetic. Then when she had to go back he was in hospital. It was unbelievable that after all the promises he had made to her, he had had a key cut to her house and gave it to a tramp and told him he could stay there. He must have hated her. He expected her to walk into the house and find herself face to face with him. However she was lucky; she knew people who lived nearby and they went round there for her, chucked him out and changed the lock on the door.

Before she had gone away, while they were going over how important it was that he didn't have anyone in, they went through one reason at a time. Firstly, they had an old aunt staying with them who had arthritis and couldn't manage keys. But it was all right, they could leave the door unlocked and she could come and go as she pleased. It was crucial they didn't get any unwanted visitors or they wouldn't be able to do that any more and the aunt would be trapped inside the house. Now that he had done that the door had to be kept locked the whole of the time, making the aunt feel either a nuisance or a prisoner. It most certainly took away her feeling of freedom. When Olive pointed this out to him, he said, 'They've gone now.'

Other people had said that. It was ignorance they could be excused for, but it wasn't ignorance with him. He knew. In fact it was one of the things they'd been through; once people like this had been it would take months to get rid of them, they would keep coming round, and indeed they did. In fact, everything they'd been through and said would happen, did happen.

She was harassed repeatedly, and then just when she would be forgetting about it all, thought she was back to normal life again, something would happen to make it all blow up again. For example, late one night she was woken up by very loud banging on the front door. Also shouting.

'Open up this door, open up this door!' came the shout. 'Police, this is the police!'

It sounded as though there were several of them and the language was dreadful. 'I'm not going to the door with this,' she thought to herself, feeling very certain her reason would be accepted. It also greatly puzzled her. Why were the police being so aggressive? Nothing very terrible had happened. It was usually after things like car chases that they started getting like this. Then suddenly she realised that it wasn't the police. She looked out of the window and only saw one man. It was only one man, very drunk, talking away to himself so she had thought there were several of them. He dashed away when he saw her face at the window.

Next day a care assistant came round. He asked James, sounding very puzzled, 'What did you invite him in for?' That's a question she later believed he should be carefully examined on. It may have been some hate for his mother which he was taking out on Olive.

Although this man dashed away so quickly at the first sight of her, she still believed he may have been the tramp who was sleeping rough at the end of the street for quite some time. Had James told him she frequently went away? Was he waiting for her to go again?

Maybe, worse than this, he'd had another man in, a bootlegger, one of those people who get cigarettes duty free on the boats going to France and make a profit by selling them cheaply. It's illegal. Once when he was in her house this bootlegger was flashing ten and twenty pound notes about, maybe in an attempt to tempt her, and to get her to go across the sea and get some for him. If so it was without success. It had the opposite effect. Large sums of money like that made her want to run.

One night she had a very bad dream. She woke James up in the middle of the night to tell him about it. Whatever for? As though he'd be interested. She must have been clutching at a straw. It would have been him who was causing the nightmares. She also suffered insomnia. That's quite common with women married to misogynists.

Another time she woke him up in the middle of the night because her address book was missing. This was very worrying with some of the characters he'd had in. It made her wonder which address some criminal had got hold of. But she couldn't get James interested. The trouble was, even if it turned up days later, she still wouldn't know if it had been out of the house and then been put back again. Maybe someone had taken down some notes from it.

She found that no agreement with him was kept for a second. That was a big shock. It reminded her of another misogynist, her cousin. He hated women, and thought they hadn't got the right to refuse or leave him and would seek revenge if they did. He promised one girl's father he would leave her alone for a month and then went round the same afternoon.

The train stopped. She was back again. She was met at the station by Elizabeth and her husband, an artist. He wasn't a very successful one, and that's the way they wanted it. Just earn and live for the day. At times he had been a street artist. Elizabeth too had been very glad to get married because of the Mental Health Act being so open to abuse. She too had had great trouble with relatives being power freaks and having too much control, but now that her husband was her nearest relative it changed everything. Her husband was very different from Olive's.

As regards facing James's mother Joyce with the fact that she had left him for over a year, she had nothing to worry about. She had not even noticed she'd gone. She hadn't been to the house once to see him during that time, not even at Christmas, and had hardly been in touch at all. They were most certainly no ordinary family.

James was indeed very bad, yet at times he would be very willing to help Olive, and in the way she wanted to be helped. Now they were together again, in the hope of being able to settle down at least in the same town, and at times even in the same house. They did at times travel about the country. Then as time went by Olive got to know his mother better and could see how she might have a son that turned out like this. A son that feared women. They do say the father is also sometimes to blame, if he is weak.

The house James had lived in for some years belonged to his family. Before that another woman had lived there and been a very good tenant from the day she was born in it, in 1901. until the day she died there in 1981. Now James was there, but he wanted to move on. He was told he had the right to, and that the house was in a trust for him. He was given assurances that if they sold it then the money raised would all be used to buy another house for him.

It wasn't surprising he wanted to go. Although some of the trouble there was his fault, he had invited some of the most dreadful oddities into the place; some of it wasn't his fault at all. For example, he'd had youths slinging bricks through his windows and shouting obscenities at him. People do that sometimes, get together in a crowd and pick on one person, especially if that person is considered a bit strange. Some of it had gone on while Olive had been in the house. She said, 'I've never been in an air raid, but this is what I call this.' She had had to duck as one window was broken and feared a lot more would go the same way.

Another time James was saying to Olive that he was going to punch them on the nose. She went out in the snow in her stocking feet to see what was going on. There was a lad of twelve there whose nose was bleeding, and his father was arguing with a neighbour. He had been throwing snowballs at his window too. She went back inside the house and said to James, 'Don't bother, someone's done the job for you.'

Another time she went out in the snow to ask them why they were doing it and they said because he was a paedophile. She said, 'What's that, what's a paedophile?' They didn't know. It was just a word you use if you want to insult someone. They said it was someone who wanked off.

So many times Olive and James did support each other; it was a dreadful shame he had this fear and hatred of women. Yet it was incurable. It reminded her of the suicide case she'd been involved in, her friend's father, where the woman had been so dreadful, not the man. People could see how suited they would have been if only she hadn't been like that.

But now he wanted to move on. The family agreed to let him sell the house. Olive never suspected why - they wanted the money. She never dreamt they would let her have complete control in selling it, but when it came to finding somewhere else for him to live, it would be they who would have control and they would make certain every house fell through.

Who were 'they'? She was not certain. She could never find out the exact legal position of the house. Who exactly were the trust and who had said what?

When the house has first been sold he had gone to live with her. But that was a very temporary arrangement. At this stage she believed that as there was so much money in the bank they would soon be able to find him somewhere else. His mother said to her, 'Now does he need somewhere else, now that circumstances have changed, now that he's got you and now that the council will find him somewhere?'

Olive found it difficult not to scream at her, 'My God! The

thought of it! Him living with me permanently!' But she did manage to say it nicely.

She went on about council flats. 'Those places are like rabbit hutches, they're so small. They're in rough areas, and once you're in one it can be very difficult to get the council to find somewhere else for you. You're stuck.'

She thought that was that. She was incredibly naive not to realise that his mother wouldn't care if anything like that happened to them and that she would fight it and try to keep the money. It wasn't that they wanted to keep their own; they were trying to get their hands on his. Ever since she had first met him she'd been told the same story, that the house he lived in was in a trust for him and through selling it they'd been told that the money would go on another house for him. They said it was in a trust to make certain he was never homeless, and now he was homeless neither Olive nor James could get hold of this money.

It was the beginning of the year, and Olive was in Kent. James had been put up in a hostel. She phoned his parents and they told her he had been visiting them a lot. His mother told her that he had said he didn't want another house. Olive thought he was just being awkward again. She didn't realise that they had been inviting him round, paying for the taxi for him, in order to get him to say this. When she got back she had it out with him. When he denied it, she thought it was some simple misunderstanding. It was still early days and she still didn't know that some people are a completely different breed and just have no feelings.

Before it was realised the family would try to keep the house, James thought he would be able to manipulate everyone by being very difficult. He thought they would stick to their duty of care and run round everywhere after him. He would do things like not turn up to see a house, and keep the agent waiting outside.

Again Olive found out that he had no interest in her safety. By now he was living in a council flat in a rough area. She had to travel late one night to make certain he turned up next morning to an appointment to see a house. It was not safe because of the drunks who were around, and on top of this she found crossing the road a big challenge. She got stuck in the middle of a big main road, with cars racing in front of her and behind, in the dark and rain, fearing that motorists wouldn't be able to see her and hit her. On top of all this she had a dog with her. She learnt that in future she should always wear bright clothes.

She arrived at the flat soaking wet and very fed up. James did make her a nice hot cup of tea and gave her something warm to eat, but next day he refused to go and look at the house for sale. He kept the agent waiting outside. So his brother and Olive agreed that as he was being like this, they would have to put an offer on the house without him seeing it. When his mother found out, she put a stop to it. She said, 'He can't have a house that he's not seen.'

It made Olive furious. It seemed as though she was trying to take charge of his life, as though she could just dictate where he would be living and he would have no say in it, and Joyce was putting a stop to it. It was more like the other way round. It was more like Olive was putting a stop to her having control over his life.

All this may sound unbelievable between a mother and son, yet there are far more dreadful families than people realize. How many people have read about Sir Winston Churchill? His parents did one unbelievable thing after another, and so did the parents of Beatrix Potter, the author of Peter Rabbit and the other children's story books.

CHAPTER 6

As time went on James's mother became more and more of an obstacle, and slowly Olive realised that she was finding the profit that had been made on the house a big temptation. James meanwhile soon realised it would suit them if every house fell through. If he was made homeless his family would enjoy being able to hang onto the money, and he began to work hard to find another one to buy. Yet it still remained a nightmare. One excuse after another was found for saying he couldn't have it.

At this time the prices of houses were rocketing. They were selling so fast the agents were no longer sending out brochures, and Olive and James would have to get up early to see which for sale notices had gone up, or to phone up the office to see what was going, and by the time they reached the house it had usually gone. They wrote to his mother explaining this, but she didn't want to understand. You couldn't get anything through to her. She wrote back explaining how to buy a house, as though Olive had never bought one before, and as though you could take your time over it. She said, 'First you must write out your needs, and then you get the agent to send you some brochures so you can see which houses have them.' But they had told her they weren't sending brochures out any more! They were selling so fast.

She then went onto say, 'This would be better than going after houses that have already been sold.' She hadn't understood that they weren't sold when they first went after them; they sold while they were on their way to see them. It made Olive sound like a fool. Did she think she was going after a house after having seen a 'sold' notice up? She later found out that thinking someone is no ordinary fool but a complete fool is a symptom of a control freak. It can be a health hazard if they've got control of the money, as it means that they have control of your life.

James' mother Joyce also kept using her other son as an excuse, saying he had to be consulted first, and that she couldn't phone him up as he was very busy, so she would have to wait for him to phone her. Olive wanted to tell her that his needs couldn't be any greater than James's and he too was her son, but she wasn't certain what the legal position was on the house and feared that if they fell out, he might lose it completely.

Indeed James had greater needs; he had nowhere to live. If he stayed at Olive's then both his mother and the council would say he didn't need a home. She would have been able to sneak him in sometimes, but he couldn't keep a secret. He'd talk about it. They'd find out he had somewhere to live.

Yet he did stay sometimes. One night it was really cold and snowing. Olive was really fed up with him, so she chucked him out. She flung his clothes out of the upstairs window and the front door shouting, 'you're not staying here!' Some of them landed on the bushes, in the public pathway at the side of the house. A taxi came for him and waited while he gathered everything up and packed it.

Olive then telephoned his mother and told her he had to have a house to live in. It didn't move her a bit. They couldn't get her out of her armchair. She was sitting on the money.

The council did find him places in hostels for the homeless, but sometimes, with some of the other residents, it can be safer to be sleeping rough than to be sleeping in one of these. And then the very worst happened; he went back to drink. Olive's heart sank the first time she got a whiff of his breath. When she told a friend of hers, 'Oh he never drinks', this friend knew that he did. She told her later how she hadn't known what to say. She had thought that if a man was drinking and his wife didn't know, she would very soon find out. And this is precisely what did happen.

It didn't budge his mother. Olive told her how he was sitting in the park on his own with a bottle of whisky and how miserable he was in hostels. She told her, for example, how the man in the next bed had been a drug addict and had died of it; James had to get up in the middle of the night and go for a walk while they came to take the body away, but this didn't move his mother. She said she suspected more of them were drug addicts, that she didn't want James to turn to drugs as well as alcohol, but most of all she emphasized that he had to have a house to live in. Yet Joyce just sat in her armchair.

Meanwhile prices of houses continued to go up and up. Soon they wouldn't have enough to buy one anyway.

A lot of people were very surprised he'd gone back to drink, as he'd been so very much against it. It had been poison to him. Yet she knew someone else like that and they'd done the same.

As regards the house, his mother would say to her impatiently, 'Leave it to me, will you?' and then do nothing, even about something crucial, like getting in a surveyor. Olive would try to get her to understand; they would think she wasn't serious if she didn't hurry up and put the house back on the market. It got embarrassing having to phone her up every day to ask her if she'd got a surveyor, only to find out she hadn't, and Olive would say yet again, 'I can easily get one in.' But sometimes she couldn't even finish what she was saying before she was interrupted with 'Leave it to me.'

Years later Olive heard how it gives some people a buzz to manipulate others, and she felt certain that this had something to do with it. Sometimes when there's a murder, the killer refuses to say where the body is. Why? Many people will assume that if you admit you know where the body is you are admitting you are the murderer, but that may not be true.

It can be nothing else but control and manipulation. One example is the Moors Murders. If Ian Brady and Myra Hindley had said where the other bodies were, they could have had concurrent life sentences, yet they still refused. The drive to manipulate overrides the desire for freedom.

But Olive knew none of this at the time, even when an agent said, 'We need confirmation that you have the money.' They would have a dreadful time getting James' mother to give that. When she phoned her, sure enough, using her other son as an excuse, she said, 'He's got a lot to do, we'll have to wait until the weekend and see if he phones us.'

Olive knew it was no good telling her how very much greater her other son's needs were and that meanwhile the house would go, because that wasn't what her interest was. Her interest was to manipulate everyone and keep the money for herself.

According to Joyce, every surveyor's report would condemn the property. Olive wanted to see them, but she wasn't allowed to. She realised no house was going to get a perfect report, and that some excuse would always be found. In one case she did manage to find that there was nothing structurally wrong with the house and it would cost about £3,000 to put right. She and James had that much between them. They offered to pay it, but were refused.

In the middle of all this Joyce bought a car worth at least £10,000. Of course that was with her money, so was her business alone, but they feared that it was because she was planning on coming into lot more money shortly when she could eventually get hold of James's. People started saying to Olive, 'If he's got money in a trust to make certain he's never homeless and he is homeless. If he can't get that money, then you should see a solicitor.' But how can you see a solicitor about your own mother-in-law? She also feared that if she did that, some other right she had might come up and she would lose more than she would gain.

Olive started writing out leaflets and putting them through people's letterboxes, saying, 'Would you like to sell us your house?' A woman phoned up and made an offer. It was one that Olive would have jumped at. She gave a price and said she could get out of her house very quickly if Olive agreed to pay it, but she couldn't. She knew her mother-in-law would muck it all up after the woman had been put to no end of inconvenience. The woman also told her, 'There's a house just across the road and two men are fighting for it'. Olive knew which house that was. She and James had rushed to get it the first second it had come onto the market, only to find it gone. Now she knew it had been put back on the market and that two men were fighting for it. James could easily beat them both with the money he had, if only he could get hold of it.

As prices rocketed James and Olive knew they should get any property, if only for a couple of years, and then, when the boom ceased, they could move again. But they also knew there was no chance with his mother; everything had to be channelled through Joyce. She began to think she would have to come to terms with it, she'd been fiddled. They'd let her go to all the trouble of selling the house, emptying it of everything, showing people round, thinking she was doing it for James, and she hadn't been doing it for him at all. She had done it so that some relative of his could have an extra car in their drive.

Then Olive and James found another house. They asked both the agent and the owner if it could be rushed through in six weeks. They said yes. Her mother-in-law then phoned her up and said, speaking slowly as though she was finding it awkward, 'Could you please leave it to me to see to, I will see to it all, as all the other houses had been such a bosh up'. Olive wanted to say, 'It's not me that's making a bosh up of everything, it's you, so that you can keep his money for yourself and you only want to be in complete control this time so that to make certain it's another bosh up.' But she couldn't. She was powerless.

When she phoned up the agent he was very offhand with her. He wouldn't say anything except 'I can't divulge that to you.' She wondered what Joyce had told him about her. Although she did indeed make a big mess of it, a much bigger one than she had ever imagined. She had the agent crawling to her. 'If you can possibly get your mother-in-law to co-operate in any way please do, we are finding her most offhand with us,' he said. Olive was very sorry to hear about it and told him so. It was dreadful. She of all people was being offhand with the agent. If it had been the other way around, how very understandable that would have been. He had run round everywhere and been most efficient, and so had the girls working for him.

Then, on the big day when it was time for the contracts to be exchanged, her mother-in-law disappeared. She had gone to see her other daughter and told no one she was going. The agent was phoning and phoning and so was Olive. Eventually she went to see if she could find her, having to change buses, a journey that would take an hour. It became clear she had gone away. She didn't dare tell the agent. It was too embarrassing. Much later when she spoke to the girl about it, to show she understood, she told her how her son, James, was nearly shouting down the phone, 'You went away the day contracts were to be exchanged, and you didn't tell anyone you were going!'

Joyce seemed oblivious to the fact it was an extraordinary thing to do. She also tried to get Olive to say she didn't want the house, no doubt in an attempt to blame her. When the girl first phoned her up and said, 'Do you want this house?' Olive thought it was lack of communication, there had been some misunderstanding in the office, so she just very firmly said, 'I most certainly do, it's my mother-in-law, it's up to her'.

'She says it's up to you.'

"What!"

Both she and James phoned his mother up and were shouting down the phone together, 'We want this house!' She told them both they couldn't have it, as it had failed the surveyor's report. After a struggle, they managed to get her to admit that there was nothing structurally wrong with it and that only about £3,000 needed spending on it. 'We've got £3,000, we'll pay for that' she said. But Joyce very firmly told them, 'No, you can't have it.'

Some people are a completely different breed. Olive used to say about the potato famine in Ireland that it was unbelievable that while the peasants were starving the landowners were putting the rent up but now she was saying it was very believable. She had seen so much of people who will do anything for money. She had no understanding of it. It was something she wouldn't do to a stranger, but how could anyone do this to her own son? Joyce knew how drink can kill someone and how it had nearly killed her son. He had nearly died of a perforated ulcer, greatly contributed to by alcohol, and if he hadn't been operated on within an hour he would have gone. She was at the hospital when it was all going on and saw him rolling about in casualty in agony. She knew that drink can be a lot more than just an unpleasant death but an agonizing one, yet nothing would move her. She remained sitting on the money after she was told he was back on the bottle and sleeping rough in the park with a bottle of whisky.

It worried Olive for some time afterwards that the woman who had tried to sell the house in the first place might try to sue the agent. She had lost money through it and been put to no end of trouble. She had arranged to go into rented accommodation, and most certainly it was the agent she blamed. She put it into the hands of another agent. Olive feared that if she should start to sue, she might be called as a witness and forced to give evidence against her mother-in-law.

Then she saw another house with another agent, one they'd dealt with before. She phoned up but when they realised who she was the girl said apologetically, 'I'm sorry but I'm afraid the agent isn't willing to deal with you.'

She was speaking in a kind voice and in any case she knew Olive was doing her best, it wasn't her who was messing everything up. But of course she also knew that Olive didn't have influence, never mind any power. Olive feared that soon there wouldn't be an agent anywhere willing to deal with them. It was the second time it had happened.

They went on trying. She tried everything. A cloak and dagger situation began, where Olive knew things about them which were confidential. Then suddenly, right out of the blue, she had a phone call from a solicitor. He told her that she could go to the agent's office and pick up the key. She couldn't believe it. She was about to question it when she realised that of course, he was the solicitor, and if he said she could then she could. They had got a house at last.

It's a story that should end happily, and up to a point it did. But

CHAPTER SIX

there were later problems because it was her mother-in-law who had the power. She could sit in her armchair and decide what had to be done, while Olive was the one left to deal with it and sometimes to even live in it. Sometimes Joyce seemed to want things to go wrong so that she could get control. Olive never felt comfortable.

There was another problem, and that was that Joyce was stupid. You couldn't get anything through to her. Although it looked as though it was her greed for money that was making her so blind, Olive later heard something else about her. During the blackouts when the Germans had been bombing London, a careful eye had to be kept on her to make sure she did not show a light. Olive could well imagine it, Joyce arguing as the planes roared over and people desperately trying to get her to understand that it was no trivial matter, the enemy would know that it was a town and drop a bomb if she turned a light on. The thought of it alone frightened Olive; she almost felt she was there, hearing the planes, but never mind, they'd soon pass over, and then her mother-in-law would put a light on. Did the other people in the air raid shelter know how lucky they were that the Home Guard were around, and they could use force? What is it that makes some people so stupid? Olive also knew of a case where a woman had to be stopped from seeing her grandchild because she couldn't understand that she was a diabetic and it would be dangerous to give her sweets.

One evening when she was going home there was a cyclist riding along the pathway, which was for pedestrians only. When he saw a pedestrian he started to ring his bell impatiently at him. Someone else on the pathway pointed out that he should be in the cyclists' lane nearby, but this just enraged the cyclist. He was so certain he was in the right. 'Some people!' A passer-by commented, and Olive wondered just how bad her mother-in-law was going to get and how dangerous it would be. Joyce certainly didn't think she was in any way

101

CHAPTER SIX

to blame for any of it, not for the delay in getting a new house or for her son going back to drink. Her conscience was completely clear. 'I just don't know what was wrong with that agent' she said. No agent could have been more efficient than he and his staff had been. People would have been amazed; it would get them thinking hard if they had known what had really happened. Yet you wouldn't have to think very hard to guess what the matter was with Joyce. She wanted the money. It was she who mucked up the sale of every house, at every stage.

After James moved in she went on, 'He'd better stay there, never in my lifetime will he move again,' and went on about all the supposed stress she had been put under. Olive had been so willing to do everything for her, yet she wouldn't allow it, and would say every time, 'Leave it to me.' Then she wouldn't get on with it but would complain at the same time about all the trouble she'd been put to.

How much right did Joyce have to say he couldn't move? It wasn't her money, it was his, yet she talked as though it was all a very big favour she was doing him. She didn't seem to think that he was her son and that it was her duty.

Olive spoke to James extremely seriously about it all. She knew how frightened he had been when living in the other house, how trapped he had felt, how desperate to get out. She had been with him when a window had been smashed. She said, 'If ever you need to move again, we'll find some way out of that, without you losing the house.'

The point was that it must never be empty. Olive would have to go and live there. They both feared that otherwise Joyce might try to sell it. But most provable of all, she said they had got less for the house he had sold than the one he bought, and she had put something towards it. Did she just tell lies or was she good at dreaming things up? There was quite a few thousand left over, which had been left in the trust should he ever need it for the house. They accepted that they'd never get that. For four years they lived there knowing how much it would change their lives if they could have a fence. They knew he easily had enough money for one, but they also knew it would be as good as impossible getting hold of it.

Then they decided to give it a try. They badly needed the fence for privacy, but far more than that they had great problems with their dog, which would get into serious fights. The neighbours also had two dogs, so it was impossible to let theirs out into the garden. He would be straight over the fence and try to savage them. Already they had had to pay a vet's bill of £400 for what he'd done to a cat. As well as this he'd been in a fight out in the street, blood everywhere, and it had involved the police. They feared they might have to have him put down. Yet in so many other ways he was adorable. It would break their hearts. If they could have a tall fence, one he couldn't jump over, it would change everything. It would mean they could leave their back door open and sometimes sit out in the back garden in privacy.

They discussed it. After all, asking for a fence was a lot less than asking for a house. They might get it with no trouble at all. They might be suffering unnecessarily. But they were proved wrong. They wished they'd never started it. They were put through a nightmare nearly as bad as the one for the house.

Joyce hadn't been to the house to see them since they'd moved in, but she turned up this time. Olive looked pleased to see her and offered her a cup of tea. She didn't want one, and said, 'I need to go out into the garden.' When she came back Olive realised what it was all about. It was to look for a reason for not letting them have a fence. She started talking about alternatives, like planting little trees. After she'd gone James and Olive agreed that they would have to wait until she was dead and then see if he could get hold of any of the savings left for him.

However, Olive decided to persevere a little, and the first time she asked her, although she said 'no' she didn't say it very firmly, so she asked her a second time a couple of months later. This time she was very firm. She went on about it quite a bit. 'It was brought up at meeting, it was discussed at length, and it was decided, no, definitely no, he can't have a fence,' she said.

Olive got quite stroppy. She knew it was James' money, no one else's. Who were these people who were saying he couldn't have it? He badly needed a fence. The only right they had was a legal right, and what is legally right can sometimes be morally wrong. Olive asked 'What meeting? Who said it, the trustees? Who are these trustees who said all this?'

Joyce wouldn't tell her, so Olive started suggesting names. 'Is it your other son? Is it your daughter? Is it the solicitor? It's very hard. It would change his life if he could have a fence.'

Her mother-in-law had drawn a picture of a big table in some posh hotel, middle-aged men all wearing suits all sitting round it and agreeing these things. Olive believed that nothing like that had happened. She believed she had dreamt the whole lot up and it was Joyce alone standing in the way, because she hoped eventually that she would get the money. They did eventually get the fence, but they both agreed, never again.

Yet something else came up. It was freezing cold and he needed a new boiler. This time there seemed to be no trouble at all. Olive didn't trust that. She wasn't living with him at the time. The house was in a dreadful mess, but when she knew the men were coming to fit the boiler she went there every day to clear it up. She spent the night there the morning before they arrived. She cleared spaces where they would need them, and made certain it was especially clear and clean by the kitchen sink. She knew they would want to brew up there. As soon as they arrived at half past seven she left, making certain they were happy and didn't need anything.

Then she received a phone call from her mother-in-law. The boss had been in touch with her, and they were happy with nothing. The two men working there were threatening to go on strike and said they couldn't be expected to work in such dirty conditions.

That was very strange, but it was never looked into. They said they wanted contract cleaners to go in. Olive was horrified. James' money was not to go on that! Was he going to be forced to spend it on such nonsense and have nothing left? Olive got more stroppy than her mother-in-law had ever seen her. 'Tell those men they can stick that right up their arse 'oles,' she fumed. She wondered how she had dared to speak like that.

She did wonder if they had seen evidence lying about the house that he had mental health problems, for example letters from doctors; it was very typical of discrimination. Or maybe they just hated their boss and wanted to spite him. Certainly it was letting him down a lot.

Then the boss telephoned her back and said he had mellowed the men and that they had agreed to do it after all. Neither Olive nor her mother-in-law were having that. They agreed that they didn't want anyone who thought they had a grievance working on it. They were told to go away. The only problem was that a £1,000 deposit had been paid.

The men then started saying they had photographs of the 'dirty mess', but Olive had been prepared for this. She immediately went straight round and got two independent witnesses to write it all down what they saw. For example, a pile of clothes in a corner were clean, not dirty. She also took photographs, although she did know that photographs alone in this case wouldn't do much good, if any.

The big point was, she had witnesses who were independent and didn't know about one another, so it couldn't be said that they had worked one another up, that was completely different from these two men. That would bear some weight.

It was crucial they knew about this. Did they also believe that as Olive's name was coupled with James's, then her word too would be considered unreliable? They may even have thought, wrongly, that she too had mental health problems. Maybe they thought, again wrongly, that she drank. There were plenty of empty bottles about, though neatly stacked up. In any case, it was crucial that they knew it wasn't their word against hers. People can get so carried away with what they think they can say and once they've done that they find it very difficult to undo.

She telephoned her mother-in-law to tell her this and to reassure her about the independent witnesses, saying, 'They are to be told at once about this, before they start losing their heads with what they are saying.' But Joyce replied, 'I don't think that would be a good idea'.

Olive was reminded again that she was stupid. You couldn't get anything through to her. She knew it was not a bit of good telling her it had been common knowledge amongst the police and everywhere else for years, that if people know there are witnesses it will help deter them, or even stop them completely from making things up. Olive was worried that in a crisis Joyce would contradict what all experts on the subject would say, the police, the mental health team and so on. This one was not a bad one, it was only a question of whether or not they'd be able to get £1,000 back, but it was reminding Olive that she would do it even if it was a question of life or death.

But it turned out all right. The community psychiatric nurse, wanted to know what it was all about. The men had said it was a health hazard, so he phoned to ask them. He had also been round to the house very recently and seen that it wasn't a mess at all. He was willing to make mention of the independent witnesses. After this the £1,000 was returned.

After they got the £1,000 back another firm very quickly did the job, very well. Yet both James and Olive found it all nerve-racking having workmen in the house, if only for a few days. They were so pleased to see them go. They put on the kettle and said, 'Good riddance to them.'

No more of that for a long time. That's what they thought. Then his mother telephoned. She said it would be a good idea to get the house decorated throughout. Both Olive and James were nearly screaming down the phone at her, 'No it wouldn't, it would be a very bad idea!' But she kept on about it.

After they'd put the phone down James said to Olive, 'She does know really.' And much later on they had reason to believe that the idea was to harass them, to get James out of the house so that they could sell it. 'Psychological warfare' as he called it, but at that time they merely kept on emphasizing that it was they who had to live in it, they who didn't mind what decorative condition it was in, and they who would be driven round the bend if painters and decorators started arriving.

But the outside of the front door badly needed painting. It was a real eyesore. There were spots of paint all over it where James had been trying to paint it himself and having DT (delirium tremens, common in drinking). As well as this the grass in the front garden badly needed cutting. It had grown very high and they were certain the neighbours didn't like it. They couldn't get the money for that.

Although Olive knew her mother-in-law couldn't go on for ever, they did wonder, if a trustee, as well as stopping you from being able to spend your money on what you wanted, could they also insist that you spend it on what you don't want? Could he not sit in privacy in his own back garden with his dog and a fence, but then be forced to have decorating which he didn't want? By the time his mother was dead, would all the money be gone?

Olive continued to wonder if it was the money and nothing else that was causing all the trouble. It reminded her that during the 1960s money wasn't lent to students to go to university; your parents had to pay and if they hadn't got it you could apply for a grant. If they did have it but refused to pay, the student would have to turn down the place and be bitterly disappointed. The assumption would be made that the parents wanted to keep the money for themselves but would that be true, or were they willing to give their children money for things that were neither asked for, wanted nor needed? At least it was their money. It didn't belong to their son or daughter and been left in a trust for their education, as with James.

They say that misogyny can originate from a dominant mother. They say it's fear of women that causes it, and Joyce was one woman Olive was scared stiff of. They were living in that house and she had all this power. She would make offers, and if they took her up on them she would back out. Did she know they would refuse when she said, 'Wouldn't it be lovely to get the house decorated throughout?'

They felt certain this was the case with other things. For example, at Christmas time, she said she wanted them to go and see her. That was difficult. It meant travelling on trains and buses, and James was afraid of some of the yobbos that hung around there. In fact, he had once been attacked by one of them. Then she said, 'I could come and pick you up in the car.'

Olive jumped at it. That changed everything. Now they could come; she said so. But then Joyce backed out and said she couldn't. It was so typical. Then about a week later she phoned again, saying she couldn't get her car to work. Olive listened. People want to talk about such things. Then suddenly she realised what she was leading up to - she couldn't give them a lift. Olive knew she didn't want them to come.

James then got himself a lady friend, Jeanette. Olive honestly didn't mind. In fact, it might be a good thing. It could mean he could annoy her instead of Olive. Jeanette was a chronic alcoholic, and her interest was not in James, it was to get money off him for drink. That didn't bother him. His interest was to manipulate a woman and this meant he could do this. Olive never stayed in the house for long if she was there; she was not someone you would choose for a friend. And there was something she did always comfort herself with; James's mother was talking about getting an injunction to stop her coming to the house. Although Olive didn't think that was necessary at the time, it was a great comfort to her to know, if necessary, that it could be done. That was until Joyce changed her mind. She had decided it wouldn't be a good idea after all. It worried Olive. It wasn't crucial, but she knew she would do it in a real crisis. It was as though she wanted to contradict everything Olive said, maybe to show her that she was in charge. She would put ideas forward, and then if Olive agreed she would change her mind. She would well and truly put a spanner in the works.

Olive started getting stomach pains and she even brought up some blood, and then she developed an ulcer. Then she had a neighbour who was throwing eggs up at her window. She felt very weak and started to think how wonderful it would be if she could stay at James's for a bit. He did sometimes have no one for a week or so, sometimes for a couple of months, and she decided to give it a try. Perhaps things would be better this time.

No chance. She couldn't get James, Jeanette or her mother-in-law interested and Joyce, instead of using her powers to stop Jeanette going to the house for a few days, simply seized the opportunity again of taking control, going on at her about all the things she'd got to do and with guarantees that it would work and started again on her about alternative medicines, saying she should have them. Everything she was saying she had to do was something Olive had already told her, and had already said she would not consider for a second.

She felt certain it was deliberate. She felt certain her mother-in-law knew what she didn't want to do so she could tell her she had to do it. Some of them were obviously designed to cause rows, to show how incapable they all were and how much she was needed.

Olive asked her, 'Do you mean you won't help me take away the cause but you will help me to live with it?' but she had to pluck up courage to say it. She feared her mother-in-law would twig that she was going into her mind, digging to find out if she wanted things to go wrong and then to take complete charge, but she had nothing to worry about; her mother-in-law hadn't got a clue. In fact she rushed forward to answer it. 'That's right, that's right, now what you have got to do is…' and continued to fire away with great enthusiasm. In other words she was saying, 'Yes that's right, I want things to go wrong so as to get control'.

Olive pleaded with Jeanette to get out. 'It's only for a few days' she said. She showed her some of the blood she had been bringing up, but nothing would move her. 'I catch two buses to get here' she would say, as though she was greatly being put on. She didn't seem to realise that this was only the beginning of a lot of people's days, in fact you frequently see them at eight o'clock in the morning down at the bus station changing buses on their way to work. But Jeanette didn't think that she should be one of them, she thought the whole world owed her a living and Olive would call her 'Your Royal Highness'.

Jeanette was very self-pitying and would whine, 'I'm an alcoholic' as though this meant she should come before anyone else. It wasn't only about the ulcer that she showed no compassion. When Olive had an emergency appointment to see her doctor about earache, it might have been an infection, which could cause sudden and permanent deafness. She said to Jeanette, 'It's not how often you are here or how long you stay, but there are certain times when I want the house to myself'. She wouldn't go. In fact it might even have suited them if Olive had gone completely deaf, because they might think Olive would be helpless against them.

Jeanette simply refused to admit that she had got to the point where it wasn't how long she stayed or how often she came that mattered but that she had to go if there was a crisis. Yet she later immediately understood when money was involved and it looked as if she might lose some. That was when the fraud squad arrived. They told her that if she stayed for more than two days a week they would stop her benefits, so she immediately stopped going for more than two days a week.

Jeanette got more benefits than Olive. In fact Olive did not get benefits, and she had far higher outgoings. For example, Olive had to pay her own council tax, while Jeanette didn't - the taxpayers paid it. Nor did she have to pay any rent, as the taxpayers paid that too. She had a nice little self-contained flat with a shared garden. The taxpayers paid for the gardener to keep it nice and they also paid for any repairs that needed doing on the flat. Yet at times it can be difficult to complain because there are some very needy and deserving cases on benefits and it would be equally scandalous if they couldn't get it.

It was strange the way Jeanette would act at caring. It was as though she knew that what she was doing was wrong. It was as if she had developed a complex about it, rather as someone who doesn't consider that they are very intelligent will talk the whole time about how clever they are, sometimes boring everyone to tears. It seemed to Olive that her mother-in-law had a complex too, that underneath it all she knew she was a hard person who had no feeling, for she too, as well as doing one thing after another to show that she had no compassion, could sound most convincing on the subject.

Jeanette said to Olive, 'I stayed away for five weeks because I didn't want to upset you'. That was either a big lie or she had completely deluded herself. She stayed away because she thought it might otherwise interfere with some of her benefits. In any case it wasn't for five weeks, and it was at a time when it would have been of no help whatsoever to Olive.

Another time, acting concerned, she said, 'Does it matter my being here?' Olive asked her, 'Why do you bother asking? If I tell you it does, you don't take any notice.'

But when the vandalism started getting worse and flowers were being smashed in Olive's front garden, she managed to find someone in Kent who would put her up. In snow and freezing weather and with a bleeding mouth she set out on a long journey across the country, feeling that if her mother-in-law did now start to show some feeling she still wouldn't trust it. She wondered how much longer she was going to be in Joyce's power, and if they were going to find she had a lot more power, for indeed she was a very powerful woman, being a trustee to that house.

After Olive had stayed in Kent a few months her ulcer got much better. But soon after her return, Jeanette started locking the door to keep her out. Olive couldn't get in, even when she had to take the dog to the vet. She would have to knock and hope that someone would hear her, which they wouldn't if they were in a drunken stupor. Yet Olive was a licensee to the house, who had a legal right, and she had good reason for needing to be in the house.

Many people will find it extraordinary that a mother-in-law stuck up for someone who would so very willingly run her son down in a real big way and get him into serious trouble, yet it came to no surprise to Women's Aid. They were quite used to someone like James having a mother like that. Olive spoke to someone there about it who said a mother will say she doesn't want her son divorced, but her real interest is that she doesn't want to have him back again.

Although according to Jeanette she had learning difficulties and was trying to get sympathy for that, she nevertheless showed great intelligence. She was well read on certain parts of the law. She would say that Olive had been threatening her, and that she knew gangsters who would beat her up. Those who know the law will know there was method in her madness. Threatening behaviour can be very serious in criminal law. It can amount to threatening someone to say they have been threatening you, and in fact, when the subject came up alongside other allegations she'd been making against Olive, the police warned her quite heavily about it. They said, 'Until now we have managed to fob her off but if she keeps on we will have no choice but to arrest you, take you down to the police station, and tape your side of the story.' It's like a young man being warned how serious it could get if a woman started making allegations of sexual assault.

Olive knew of course that she would get no support from her mother-in-law on this. She wouldn't care if anything like this happened and it would be a waste of time trying to get her to do anything to help prevent it, like getting Jeanette stopped from coming to the house. If the worse did happen, and if Olive was arrested, she might even be pleased about it; it would show how hopeless Olive was at managing and how much she was needed. It upset Olive very much, as she had been born into a family with so much care, a family that would be horrified at the thought of anything like this happening to anyone, and would give them their full support and do their best to prevent it. She found it very difficult to come to terms with the fact that all families were not the same.

Jeanette could mean business all right; she had once got a man arrested on suspicion of rape.

James and Jeanette were not having a love affair; they were both having an affair with alcohol, and for other reasons Olive was not a bit jealous. Yet Jeanette tried to make out that this was the only problem, not the ulcer, because it was likely to be believed. She was most hypocritical the way she would talk about it in the name of caring. Sounding as though she was truly concerned, willing to admit that up to a point she might be in the wrong, she would slowly say, as though she was studying it at the same time, 'I wonder if I should have...' And so on.

Olive would say, 'Come off it Jeanette, you know very well I'm not jealous, you just need an excuse to do nothing in the name of caring', and yet it frightened her. It's extraordinary how people will do this and get away with it. We are indoctrinated into believing we should have feelings for one another, and that is considered admirable. Did Jeanette believe herself that the only problem was that Olive was jealous? The only thing she ever did wrong was not to handle this jealousy properly.

Did Jeanette really see herself as a compassionate person who was sincerely concerned about this? If so it was quite extraordinary, as she was in truth such a hateful person.

As time went by Jeanette continued to insist that Olive had made these threats, and had said she had friends who were gangsters who would beat her up. Olive could never make up her mind; did she imagine she was going to brainwash her into believing that she did say it, something so bizarre and out of character, or is it that false beliefs are fixed? Whichever it was, it was quite extraordinary. It was also an eye opener to Olive that anyone could make such a statement, something so very wildly untrue, yet it was obvious what her motive was. She didn't want Olive in the house. James was on good money, his disability allowance, and Olive might try to stop her getting it. It is quite well-known that people on disability allowance attract the scroungers, and now Olive had found that it could also attract someone who was quite evil.

Jeanette also tried to get Olive to believe that although Olive had said it, she had forgotten. Looking at her, as though she was concentrating, going into it deep, as though to get the truth out, she was slowly saying, and quoting the actual words, 'No you must have forgotten but you did, you said you knew gangsters who you can get to beat me up.'

All this got Olive thinking deep. It worried her. When she saw in the news these people in the dock, did they do the crime or was it just a witness's fantasy? She now knew that people make statements without a grain of truth in them. She said that you shouldn't be on a jury until you are 35 or you won't know what lies some people can tell, but when you are 70 you are too old. You know too much and you'll have everyone acquitted.

Olive's mind went back to the days before all this had started, and she had never really given it any thought. Jeanette had telephoned her at five in the morning. It was a mad, mad call and she'd said, 'Have you got a man friend who's got a gun and is going to shoot me?'

'Don't be absurd' Olive said.

'Only James pointed at a man in a coffee bar and said, 'You see that man over there? He's got a gun and Olive is going to pay him to shoot you."

'Don't be so ridiculous' Olive said.

Jeanette then started talking about how she wouldn't be able to come round to the house any more if Olive was going to do that, but in those early days Olive didn't really give it a lot of thought and merely put the phone down. Now she wondered. Was she getting it tape-recorded, and with promises to keep away, was she hoping she would be able to egg Olive on to make these threats? Did she intend to blackmail her in some way or at least get some kind of a hold on her?

She had done something else that Olive had found quite worrying. She had said, 'Only you have a lot of money, you could so very easily pay someone to do that'. Olive was certain she was threatening her. She had told her again and again how was she was only in the basic tax bracket and that it wasn't safe for her to spread this rumour around. She was afraid of her house being broken into. In fact she had said she was afraid of waking up in the middle of the night and finding a drug addict there.

Sometimes things ran smoothly along, but it would never last. Next time work was needed on the house they decided to pay for it themselves. There wasn't much left in the trust now, and it certainly wasn't worth risking a fight for. But he continued to do one thing after another which suggested misogyny was the problem. In a letter to the Mental Health Team, she wrote:

Is there any chance he can be assessed for this? For example, although I don't mind at all doing all the housework, he insists upon forcing it upon me and making me do it in a way I don't want to. It's got to be done in a way he knows I will object to very strongly.

For instance, we had workmen in this weekend. I was very happy to clean everything up before they came, but I am certain of it; it was with malice that he invited his lady friend Jeanette there for the same weekend, told her she could stay for the weekend, that it was his house, and that it didn't matter what I said.

He's had this woman friend for some time. I honestly don't care. I have been in the house before when she's been there. But I never stay long.

Regardless of who she was, I would find her continual chatter and other things unbearable. He knew I would find it impossible to work round her, to have her in the way the whole of the time, the house is unliveable when she is in it, I am driven mad within five minutes. He knows this.

Clearly he was planning on having a very stormy weekend with one row after another. It didn't happen. I left immediately after she arrived, leaving the house dirty for when the workmen arrived.

Before I went, he was saying what time he and Jeanette were going out, and what time they'd be back. That would mean certain things would have to be done within a certain time and I wasn't having that. I want to be able to stop and have a cup of coffee when I want to, and not depending on what they're doing. If it was something that couldn't be helped I wouldn't mind but it wasn't. It was deliberate. It was to make me work in a certain way and in a certain time, and again, it would be something he knew I would object to very much.

But he didn't clean it up. It was left dirty and I am certain of it, his attack on Friends of the Earth was a vicious one and was partly directed at me. He knows I am very keen on recycling. He did throw out some perfectly good apples that I had spent some time stewing and put them into the deep freeze. He did throw out a big pile of newspapers which were going to be recycled, and he did go out to buy some black bin liners to put the rubbish bin, although I have carefully explained to him not to do this. I have already got a cupboard full of them. I have opened it up several times to show him. I have said to him every time, 'Please, this house is so full of junk, and I am trying to steadily get through it, please only use these.'

The first time he went out to buy some more, I went cold all over. I knew he had done it on purpose to spite me. Why does he hate me?

Those were the only three things he did to clean up. The idea being, 'If you don't do it, and you've got to do it in a way you object to very strongly, then I'll do it, and that will be in a way that will upset you very much.' He hates me.

When we were living in Kent, he was putting rubbish into a skip which a man across the road had hired. This man objected very much, saying how much he had paid for it, and that it must not be filled up with other people's rubbish. James refused to take this seriously and went on putting rubbish into it, causing me great embarrassment. This included a kettle which had nothing wrong with it.

When we lived in the north he was doing things which I feared very much would cause bad relations with the neighbours. At one time, I thought I would have to go to the front door and face them with it and say, 'I am very sorry, but I can't do anything about it, I have told him not to do it and he doesn't take any notice.'

I have tried to let him see I accept him as boss, but the trouble is, it's got to be in a way I object to. When a man came to ask about painting the front door I said I wanted it white. James said he wanted it red. So I laughed and said to this man, 'Then it's got to be red, I'm only second in command in this house.' However, next day when the man arrived to do it, I couldn't stay. James had invited Jeanette round, and was planning on having a row going on while he was doing it.

Very seriously indeed there is no thought for me. There is no concern that to be in a place where there is row after row could make me very ill. When my mouth has been bleeding with an ulcer I have shown it to both Jeanette and James. I've told them how ill it could make me. I told them how I was getting earache, that I feared an infection could lead into permanent deafness and that stress was greatly contributing to it, but neither of them will budge. 'I'm not going,' she will say, 'I catch two buses to get here'. That's even though it's very rare she's asked to go.

After Olive posted this something else happened that she wished she could have mentioned. His drinking had got very bad, and while being very much in this state, the woman next door had come round to say she suspected there was a rat in her house, and had he seen any in his? He said, 'I've got a rat, it's in my trousers.' Olive is certain that gave him a very big buzz, truly he could insult a woman with that. She quietly went away. Clearly he was very, very drunk.

As regards vermin, there was none of that in the house. No one left food about and they were all aware of what not to do, and kept to it. There were rats at the bottom of the garden as it backed onto a railway line, but they never came up to the house. They most certainly never came inside. Maybe with houses these days they can't.

When James had first gone back to drink, she thought for a while that it was only social drinking, for he seemed to be managing all right. Yet people told her, 'If he used to be an alcoholic and now he's drinking again, it's going to finish up in one disaster after another.' How right they turned out to be. It reached a stage where he was drunk every night, every morning, every evening and then every night again. Don't ask where the money was coming from for all this, that's something that's always been a mystery to others when a person is drinking.

She didn't have to live with him, but she needed to go to the house quite often because of the dogs. She had one and so did he, and he adored them. He was a very good dog sitter, but at the same time he badly needed a helping hand with them. It is well known with misogynists that they will use pets to control the woman, and she sometimes wondered at times if he was doing this. Yet he would never threaten to be cruel to them. He would do one thing after another to show how much he loved them. She wondered why. Maybe he had a true confidence that a dog could never hurt him, and didn't fear them as he did women.

Olive once needed to take the dog to the vets. It was very difficult to get inside the house, as he had such undesirable characters there and she was frightened to meet them. She also had a bad back, and it was difficult having to lift the dog even though it was very small. In the end she took it away completely. She said that while the dog was ill he would have to stay with her. This greatly enraged James.

Then she had a phone call from one of the down-and-outs, Ian Hill, who had moved into the house. He went on at her, finishing up with, 'And if he commits suicide it will be your fault.'

She knew something about this sort of thing; sometimes when a person accidentally kills themselves it's been investigated to see if its murder. She suspected he intended spicing up his drinks. She told the police, and asked if it could be regarded as a threat to kill. They said it couldn't. They also said, and said it very nicely, 'If it's his house he can have whoever he likes in it.'

But it wasn't his house, not entirely. Olive had some legal rights. She could even go and live there permanently if she wanted. The police listened and then said if she could produce a document saying so, for example a lease, then that might be helpful. Things can sometimes be left to police discretion.

The trouble was, this would have to be first channelled through her mother-in-law and that could cause a lot of aggravation. When she phoned her and asked for it, she was promised it but it was then followed by a game of donkey and carrot. She was told, 'Don't stick your oar in, the solicitor is sorting it all out.'

Sorting all what out? Although she had said that the only thing that was needed was a copy of the lease to the house she had nevertheless asked for something else. She'd wanted to contact the other two trustees to the trust, yet she even had trouble being certain who they were. She did write a note to one of them and asked her mother-in-law to pass it on, but she refused. She wanted to be the only one who made decisions. Olive later found out that this was very much out of order, it was in breach of any trust and it reminded her so much of something else. That was when she'd been shocked by what a social worker was doing; she discovered that some of it was not just abuse of the Mental Health Act, but in breach of it.

However, yet again she had to accept it that her mother-in-law was in complete control as she telephoned her every day for the next three weeks saying how very urgent it all was and telling her how dangerous it was for her son to be in the house with those people. Indeed it was, as people there were having some of the most dreadful rows. They were all crawling about the floor very drunk and throwing aspirins, paracetamol and other drugs, all legal but all very dangerous. Olive said to the police, 'I daren't go round there. I can see an accidental death, and me being under suspicion for murder.' They didn't deny this could happen.

She remembered the case of her friend's father's suicide, when she and her mother had been called out in the middle of the night. The police checked up - did he tell anyone he had taken this overdose? It was lucky he had, otherwise his wife would have been under suspicion, but he had telephoned his son in law and said he'd taken it. In this same case the hospital had been very concerned about tablets being chucked about all over the stairs, the hall and so on. They spoke to Olive and her mother very seriously about it, saying his wife should not go back to a house like that. They could see her taking them all. Both Olive and her mother reassured the nurse they'd see to it, but when they got back the police had been round and cleared it all up.

Remembering all this, Olive continued to remind her mother-in-law that she had been promised a copy of the lease of the house, and Joyce kept telling her she'd let her have it. Then after three weeks of this game of cat and mouse, she told her she'd changed her mind; she'd decided not to give it to her after all. She said she would write to her son and these visitors herself and explain to them what the legal position was, but what she sent them was rubbish. They wouldn't take any notice of that, and how would the police know it wasn't a hoax? It wasn't on headed notepaper, and in fact one document wasn't even in handwriting. It was typed out with no address on it and no signature. It was something that Olive could well do without. It might well go round a pub and be jeered at.

Olive told her again how she feared this man was going to spice up her son's drinks and questions were going to be asked about murder. She went into detail about some of the rows they were having and the drugs she'd seen them throwing at one another, but nothing would move her mother-in-law. She just said, 'It's his life and if he chooses to lose it it's up to him.'

Olive wondered how many thousands she might think she would get if he did. Did she think she'd get the house back again if this happened? It was worth quite a bit by now.

In any case, under the Mental Health Act he was not free to squander his life as he liked, especially if there was a danger that he might accidentally kill himself. The Mental Health Team could intervene, especially if the nearest relative was concerned. If any relative had the right to make such a statement (which they didn't) it should be Olive, his wife. Yet in this case it was his mother, as she was a trustee to the house.

Someone else said about her, 'She seems to be trying to kill him off.' Then another thing happened to enrage Olive. The doctors had refused to speak to her on grounds of confidentiality, even though he had given written consent and she had delivered it by hand; even though she was his nearest relative and was seeing him every day. However they did speak to his mother. Maybe too many doctors were involved. Maybe the left hand didn't know what the right hand was doing.

After Joyce told her, 'No, I'm not going to let you have the lease' Olive took the dog out for a long walk. She must have walked nearly all night. She comforted herself with one thing - her mother-in-law might not live much longer, and she was not sorry about it. In fact her being out of the way would come to her as a relief. She decided that in future, at the end of every day she would comfort herself by saying, 'One day less of living in fear of her.'

Maybe the most astounding thing of all was when Joyce said that everything was in perfect order. This was at a time when they were all crawling about the floor drunk, having a big row and throwing drugs at one another. Some people might think she was saying there was nothing you could do about it and you might as well leave them to it, but not so. She had previously said that a solicitor was sorting it all out, and maybe she intended to justify it with that, yet Olive very much doubted that she had consulted any solicitor.

More than ever Olive felt it was giving Joyce a buzz to be able to manipulate her like this, to have her on the phone to her every day to ask 'Have you done it?' (whatever it was that needed doing). Olive's most recent request was for a copy of the lease to the house, and she was told every day that she could have it tomorrow, but tomorrow never came. Joyce said she had changed her mind and decided not to let her have it after all, and the next day she went away on holiday to the continent, leaving her son. How could she? Olive telephoned her solicitor and asked, 'Is there any way we can insist that the police help us?' She was told there wasn't. This man hadn't actually said he was going to kill him. It was left to police discretion.

Olive put the phone down and sat in the armchair in deadly silence. She wanted to put her head in her hands and cry. She stayed there for ten minutes coming to terms with it. She had decided to get up and make herself a cup of tea, to try to forget all about it, when there was a knock on the door. Two police officers were standing there. 'What do you think we should do about it?' one of them asked.

She had just spoken to her solicitor, so she knew what was reasonable and realistic. She told them, 'If you just say something to suggest to Ian Hill you are suspicious then I think that alone might deter him.'

They went round to James's to see him. Ian Hill went running out of the back door when he saw them coming, and she didn't see him for a long time afterwards. It had worked.

After James's mother came back from her holiday it took her over a week to phone up and find out how he was. In fact he had been in hospital, not with an overdose but with suspected fits. That happens to people who are drinking; it begins to affect the brain. James and Olive decided not to tell her. When Joyce found out she said, 'I want to know if he's been in hospital.'

But why? Maybe to look caring or in the hope of getting more control this way. But did she have the right to know if she would do nothing to avoid it? Olive asked the community psychiatric nurse, a new one called Nurse Spooner. Nurse Spooner said, 'Well she would wouldn't she?' It's a normal assumption to make for someone who knows nothing about the case or is completely untrained, but Nurse Spooner was neither of these and it was a very strange thing for her to say.

Olive later spoke to James about it quite seriously. She said, 'We may have problems with that'. Nurse Spooner later said something else which was worrying. 'It's such a shame when family don't agree about a relative's care,' she commented.

Was she really so pathetically naïve? There was much to suggest that their interest was in the money, and that they had no interest in his care.

Although it's true that the Mental Health Act is very open to abuse, it can give the relatives quite a bit of power, especially if they make the claim that their interest is in the patient, *many* people think this doesn't really matter as long as no member of the team say they believe it. Once they do, if anything like that starts up, that patient's life may begin to be a nightmare. They no longer have the control they should.

Olive wondered if Nurse Spooner had anything to do with the doctors only being willing to speak to his mother and not to her. Was there something sinister going on? She wondered if she should ask the doctors to take into consideration, when deciding who was free to die, who would be thousands of pounds better off.

Then Nurse Spooner, with no good reason, refused to consider that James might be a misogynist. She said quietly, 'Now if he was one then he would hate me, and he doesn't hate me'.

Olive was quite shocked at such ignorance from a psychiatric nurse. A misogynist doesn't necessarily hate all women; he may only hate those who come into a certain category. A little later she made a similar remark, and Olive concluded that she wasn't ignorant but in denial. However, with James's help she managed to get rid of her. He had another nurse after that.

As regards Ian Hill, he did come back into their lives some years later and it showed more than ever that Joyce's interest was in the money. Firstly, when he was visiting the house she said it would be all right for him to come and he could stay as long as he liked as long as he paid some rent and she started trying to get some housing benefit from him. She then started trying to get some for her son James and took no notice when she was told time and time again that she couldn't have it because he was family, and that it was a family home he was in.

Then there was more trouble, because Ian Hill started openly making threats to kill Olive. She told the police. They came up to the house to see her about it and then went round to see the two witnesses who had heard him say it. They said, 'Oh it's not just Olive, he's got a list of people he's going to kill', so the police went round to see him about it and to get the list. He disappeared for some time after that, but then he turned up in a nursing home. Everyone hoped he would never come out, but he did. He went straight round to see James. Joyce started up again saying she wanted some rent off him and also off James, and when she was told again that they wouldn't pay it she said, 'They will do when they find out that if they don't they will have to find somewhere else for him to live'. She could only have meant by this that she intended throwing him out.

Then Ian Hill died. Olive was in the house when it was all going on. He looked dreadful, like a victim in a concentration camp, and he started having fits on the floor. 'Get him out of here!' she said to James. He called an ambulance, but Ian Hill hadn't been in the casualty department long before he discharged himself.

'Don't let him into the house' she said to James when he arrived back, but James did let him in and he started having more fits. A taxi came for him but refused to take him, so James called for another ambulance.

'They're not having this, going to and fro all night for him' said Olive. But the ambulance did come for him, and he died in it.

As time went by it became more and more of a worry that James would invite just anyone into the house. One woman, a drug addict, took Olive's post office book. It had six hundred pounds in it. At least the woman didn't get the money.

The house continued to be a dreadful mess, empty bottles and beer cans all over the floor as well as cigarette ends. Yet some of the people who went in weren't all bad and there would be long periods when he would have no one in at all. It was during one of these breaks that someone very nice came to stay, Ronald. He had been one of Dr.

Barnardo's boys, but now he lived in a rough area, so he found it a safe haven.

Ronald was determined to earn his stay. He cleared up the house from top to bottom, got new curtains and put flowers in the window.

Then Olive had a call from him. He had found out what James was like. He couldn't believe how bad he was. He told her how James had come home with a heroin addict he had met at the bus stop and Ronald wasn't sleeping in the same house. He could see himself being strangled in his sleep. Olive agreed it was as bad as some of the hostels. It was safer to spend the night in a shop doorway than in some of them.

One night she had a phone call from James, who said he was going to be out all night and could she go to look after the dog. She went very willingly and settled down there for the night. Then James came in. She thought he had merely changed his mind. Then she heard him talking on the phone; he was inviting other people round. Clearly it was open house for anyone. She wouldn't be able to stay in that house all night with any of them. He told her she could sleep in the room upstairs, but she could not. She would feel trapped up there. She began to plead with him, 'Please don't have them in, I can't walk home now at this time of night,' but he wouldn't have it. Through lonely lanes, at closing time for the pubs, terrified of the drunks, she had to go.

What did he do that for? To show off to everyone that he had a wife that had to accept what he said. He liked an audience. She suspected as well that he intended to play music, to make her come down every few minutes to say she couldn't bear it and he was going to show everyone how she had to accept what he said. They hadn't spoken to one another on the phone for over a year. She would rather they never spoke at all than wonder when he would be willing to speak and when he would put the phone down on her.

One day she had a phone call from his mother. James had telephoned Joyce to say the dog was ill. She had acted as a go between before. She started talking about a charity that would pay the vet bills. Olive was horrified. It was one they paid into, and they weren't going to start taking out. In any case, they weren't on income support and the charity wouldn't pay unless they were. Joyce wouldn't accept this and started questioning it. Olive wondered what her motive was. Why did she want to know about their financial affairs?

Then she told her to phone James about it. 'He'll be in now,' she said.

'Yes, but he won't speak to me on the phone.'

'He will if you phone him now.'

Olive wasn't accepting that he would only speak when it suited him. She wished she would keep out of their marital affairs. 'Well I can't go on being a go between,' she said.

Olive didn't want her to in any case, but it was about the only thing she had ever done that had in any way been useful. It was something that would only take a minute or two, and which was only asked of her every few months. Was she asking a price? Was she saying, 'I want some control or I won't do it'?

Olive then went to see what it was about. She found the dog perfectly healthy, skipping about like a puppy. It seemed her mother-in-law had been making a mountain out of a molehill. He had said very little about the dog being ill. She wondered why. Did it worry Joyce if they spent a lot of money on vet bills? Or was it simply to get control and nothing else?

Yet it wasn't any of this that made Olive decide to leave him for a second time. Her mother-in-law was very keen on alternative medicines. Neither Olive nor James believed in them, yet she would go on and on about them. It would drive Olive mad, and after a bit she wasn't listening any more. She would hold the telephone receiver away from her ear.

One day when she was going on at James like this, Olive wanted to say, 'Now stop this, he's TOLD you, he's not interested.' This was when they were just setting out to see her. She felt like saying they wouldn't come at all if she was going to do this, but of course this was what Joyce wanted.

When they arrived, they found she had made an appointment for him to see a 'quack', as she referred to the doctor. Olive was quite surprised James didn't start shouting, and it was certainly an appointment he could be excused for not keeping. If she had done that alone Olive would soon have forgotten about it, but there was far more to it than that. She believed she had made him fear women by doing things like this when he was very young. After this, and maybe because of it, the man insisted that any appointments could only be made by the person themselves.

The question of 'quacks' came up again when Olive was ill. Having forgotten about all this she decided to give it another try. Maybe now that she wasn't well, her mother-in-law would be willing to understand she was not to have stress and be willing to help lessen it. She went into some detail on everything. Firstly her earache. She had an appointment to see the emergency doctor that day, and feared she might have some infection that could cause permanent deafness. Secondly she had a bad leg, could hardly walk at times, and might have to go into hospital for an operation. She said it was crucial she didn't have a lot of stress and that the ulcers she kept getting in her mouth weren't helping. She told her that to have a continually ulcerated mouth could finish up with cancer.

Later that day Joyce called her back again. She said, 'I've been thinking about how I can help you. I can pay for you to see Mrs Rochester.'

'I don't believe in alternative medicines.'

This was not accepted. Joyce went on and on, and Olive held the receiver away from her ear.

'I can hardly walk at the moment, it would take me three hours to get there and back,' she said, and then Olive did begin to take some notice. There was a man just round the corner who did the same things, so she said, 'Oh yes, I will be able to go and hardly have to walk at all' and she told her about the other 'quack'. But her mother-in-law wouldn't have it. She wasn't paying for that. Olive could only go if she went to the one she recommended. Yet she never offered her a lift there, even though she did drive a lot. It all frightened Olive very much; people whose interest wasn't to help but to get control, and they would even do so in the name of caring.

In the middle of all this someone was trying to get through. Olive kept saying so, 'I've got to go,' but she wouldn't let her. She just kept on saying, 'Let them wait.' Olive wondered if she should just put the phone down on her. She suspected it was someone who was willing to help her in the way she wanted to be helped. Did her mother-in-law suspect this too? Did she deliberately block the line because she wanted to be the one in charge?

Next came some bad news from London. Madame Paree's husband was dead. Olive phoned her. It was so like life; they had been so happy together. It seemed that only the unhappy marriages lived on. She told her how they had met. Some men might need women and fear them, but they could cope with the combination of both. He'd been one of them. He had received a letter through his letterbox asking for tools. They were sent to the developing world. As after his father had died he had been wondering what to do with them, he telephoned this number.

'So many times I have had to pluck up courage to telephone a woman and ask her, 'Yes, or no, will you go to the flicks with me?" he said. He never dreamt that this time he was phoning a woman who would say, 'Yes, I will marry you'.

Now she had to think about how to face the world without him. One good thing; it seemed they were going to change the law on letting, so it would shortly be easier to get tenants out. The woman who owned the shop across the road was also rejoicing about it. She'd had a flat above the shop empty for several years, and it would be wonderful if she could let for the next five as she was planning on going abroad. She had intended to brick it up as she had been advised about squatters getting in, but now there would be no need for it.

It hadn't always been completely empty. Her daughter who worked in the shop from time to time had lived there for a while. That was typical; if a flat was let, it was to someone who didn't really need it. Her eighteen-year-old daughter could so easily have stayed at home. She had only been allowed to have this flat because it was better than leaving it empty.

People were aware that buying to let can push up prices of houses and make it impossible for some people to buy, but none of this justified the extent the government went to over it. It stopped nearly all letting, so much so that many people who wanted to rent could no longer find anywhere.

When Olive arrived back she found everything much as she had left it. The basement was now empty and she immediately moved in. There were two other girls in a bed sitter upstairs. One of them was Clare.

CHAPTER 7

CLARE

Clare felt sick. She told the story of a house she'd just been to in a road in Dover called East Cliff. It was cold and empty, the house her mother had died in; a terraced house facing straight out onto the pavement and next to a pub. She had been away for a while and when she came back she went cold all over the first time she stepped outside.

As she began to walk down the road she could see the face of a man in the pub next door staring out at her. It was the face of someone who made her blood run cold, a man she did not consider human; a man who was sick. As she walked down the road she could feel his eyes on her back and sure enough when she looked back there he was, standing at the front door of the pub still looking out at her. He waved and she waved back, as she was afraid to do anything else.

This man's interest wasn't in her at all, and she had no understanding of it. When her mother had just died and she had returned from a long journey tired, cold and hungry his only interest had been to get her into bed. Yet she was a woman with a heart full of compassion and if it had been the other way about, if someone else had arrived after a long journey bereaved, cold and hungry, it would have been her pleasure to welcome them and to make things comfortable and cheerful.

Her mother had been ill for a long time and she had needed to visit her and nurse her. She had no one to help her, no brothers, no sisters, but she picked up nursing as she went along. Sometimes she'd take her mother back home with her, but leaving the house empty so much had created such problems, and it had been a big worry to her. If only she could find someone reliable to look after it while they were away. She was perfectly willing to pay someone, but she had been let down. People wouldn't help in the way she wanted them to. This man Lee was one of them.

At first he had not been willing to send on her post in the way she wanted. All she had asked him to do was to cross off the address on the envelope and put on the stickers she had provided for him. She told him that it didn't matter if it was junk mail, just send it on and let her decide. But he wouldn't do it.

The first time she realised this was when he phoned her and told her he had been to the house and collected her mail. But why was he keeping it? He then started going through the envelopes one at a time saying, 'Shall I send this on?' Why couldn't he just send the lot on?

Yet she knew nothing about misogyny and the men who want to control women. Patiently she waited while he went through the letters. She was later to discover that she was lucky he had even done that. At times he had sent it back with, 'No longer living at this address' written on it.

But on this night some time ago, this very cold night, she had never thought it would get as bad as it did. She had gone to his house to see if he could help her with the heating, which wouldn't work. He started making smutty jokes to her about it, and her heart sank. She just stood there looking very serious. She pretended not to understand. He did pop down the road and get the pilot light on for her but he wasn't willing to leave it as a simple favour. He asked her for a kiss. She refused. She felt sick. What a time to ask her when everything was going so wrong and at a time when she was so dependent on him! Of course she refused and realised in future she would just have to freeze. He was repulsive.

Yet he still came round to the house. One night she left her door open for a minute while unpacking some things when suddenly she heard his voice. He was standing behind her. He had been drinking and was ready for an argument. She was glad she had her dog with her. In fact he was using the dog as an excuse to be in the house, saying she wasn't looking after it properly. She did not know that people who do that sometimes use pets to control someone. He was cross-examining her on the dog's care, how did she feed him etc. He finished up with, 'Well I'm very sorry but you can't manage.'

She knew that as well as wanting to 'manage' things for her, to take charge, he was feeling resentful because she had refused to go to bed with him. She kept looking up to heaven and reassuring her mother, 'Don't worry Mum, I'm taking no notice of this.' How keen her mother had been that she ignored such people, whether they were viciously jealous or what.

But Clare felt that her mother was with her the whole of the time. They say it's not unusual for someone who is bereaved to have a vision and since her mother had died she had seen her. Her face had been full of compassion.

On the night when she felt she could feel his eyes on her back she continued to walk with her dog to the end of the road, a sweet little side street with hanging baskets and cliffs in the back ground. She crossed the road and was by the sea. She could see boats coming across from France, hear the gulls, everything that could be so pretty, but what was there left for her? Nothing.

She was very afraid of this man. He had also shown signs of being jealous of other men. One day while he was away, she had got another man to go inside the house for her to see to something, and when Lee found out he phoned her and said as if was some emergency, 'Someone else has been inside that house!' He did not accept that this was perfectly in order. He was behaving like a dog after a bitch on heat who had smelt another dog. Clare had to remind herself that there were quite a few nice men about as well; she was not to generalize about them or hate them all.

She could see herself getting raped. So often it is a man the woman knows, and so often, in fact maybe always, it's not a sex crime but a power one. He definitely wanted control.

She continued to walk along the sea front. Everything could be so lovely. It was a clear night and she could see France across the water. She dreamt of being able to escape there. She didn't think of going to the top of the cliffs and throwing herself off, although they were so near and she could get up there within a few minutes. Yet she was beginning to understand why some people did it.

Then she telephoned a friend. They gave her the phone number of Madame Paree and said it was a bed and breakfast place for battered women. It was late at night when Clare phoned her, and Madame Paree took the call. She was amused that her house was being considered a refuge.

Clare got the first train from Dover Priory railway station the next morning. She locked the house up completely. She didn't care any more that the house wouldn't be looked after; she felt very depressed.

That night Clare dreamed that she was under sentence of death. She had travelled back to the 1960s, when the death penalty was still in force in England and you would be given three clear Sundays before your execution. She dreamed she was in a cell which was so comfortable that you could call it a bedsitter. She could go out into the short corridor outside where there were rooms; they all had a few pieces of furniture, yet no one was in them. The prison officers were more like nurses, young girls who were so kind and gentle. That was all she saw. They seemed sincerely sorry that she had lost her appeal and kept giving her words of comfort by saying that right up to the last moment the Home Secretary might give her a reprieve. 'You never know what might come up,' they told her.

Then, in her dream, the day of execution came. It was nine o'clock in the morning and the prison officials marched her out to be hanged. Yet they were going in the wrong direction; they turned left instead of right. They opened a door wide. They were letting her out. She was faced with open spaces, garden, fields and woods.

'We'll just have to hope it gets overlooked that we didn't carry out the execution' said one of them.

But how was she going to manage? It reminded her of the wilderness at the end of her road in East Cliff, just up the steps on the white cliffs of Dover. How often she had walked amongst all that, completely bewildered, and in this dream she was back again in this world, this wide and wicked world. She knew no one; she had no support.

When Clare awoke she wondered what had made her have such a dream, and yet it was how she felt. People who hate humanity make people suicidal and she sometimes felt she was putting herself under sentence of death. When they brought her out of that cell, she didn't really want to decide for herself if she should turn left or right because both ways were so formidable.

Madame Paree was reminded again that her house had become a

refuge when a battered man arrived, brought by her nephew. The two of them stayed in the house some time. He had the room in the attic and was very quiet, so they only knew he was there if the nephew was cooking for two. They would call him Mr Naylor as he reminded them of a nice man of that name. Why is it, if it's the man that's battered, if only psychologically, that jokes are made about it? In comics you see a wife with sleeves rolled up and a rolling pin. Yet some women do terrible things. The one most heard about is to use the children to control the man. Usually the woman gets custody.

CHAPTER 8

JENNIFER

Jennifer had done her training to be a driving instructor and failed the tests twice. But just as she'd decided she didn't want to do it, she was going to give it all up, she passed. She didn't know what to do. She wanted to work for someone, so she got a job in a ladies only driving school which belonged to a Miss Smith. The trouble was, with various legislations they were bringing in about sex discrimination they weren't allowed to accept women only. Yet Jennifer never minded teaching a man to drive. Maybe that's why Miss Smith employed her.

There had been blow-up after blow-up over Miss Smith's Ladies Only Driving School. She was told she wasn't allowed to do it. Every time there was a complaint about it, she would teach a man to drive and say that she didn't mind men, but they didn't often ask for lessons. It was pointed out to her how coincidental it was that every time they did ask, she was booked up.

CHAPTER EIGHT

At times she would be openly declaring what she was doing. For example, in the waiting room while someone was out taking their test, she would go on and on about it, saying 'I'm not going to teach a man to drive.' This would be in front of other driving instructors, all men, and as Jennifer once said, 'The examiners must be able to hear it too.' They would indeed hear it if they were in the next room, where they would be if someone hadn't turned up to take a test. If Miss Smith got really hot under the collar she would have something to attack them back with. It had been alleged that some of the driving examiners were sexist. She'd heard it said that it the young girls all passed first time.

'More women examiners are needed here' one man told her. 'They'll keep the girls in check.' The trouble there was of course that the men would all start passing first time.

Eventually the complaints got so many that Miss Smith decided to take early retirement. Jennifer thought of applying to be an examiner. It was no more difficult than being an instructor, and it was a job where you either said 'yes' or 'no.' As one man put it, 'If when the examiner gets up his wife is feeling amicable and he get a bit, then you've passed your test.'

Jennifer didn't like disappointing people, and they were very disappointed when they didn't pass a driving test. In any case, an examiner doesn't have the same power as an instructor. He can't tell them what to do. He has to get out and walk back if it starts getting dangerous. Some people turn up to take the test when they are nowhere near the standard. They know how to stop and start a car and that's about all. Yet quite often it's not they who cause the trouble. Sometimes when someone hadn't passed they had it so bad they had to call the police. One examiner stopped using the expression, 'Swearing like a trooper' and started saying instead,

'Swearing like a woman.' He said it was they who taught him a few new words.

A driving examiner is not supposed to be chatting to the candidate, it's a boring job just sitting there in silence, but then some of these examiners can be very naughty. When Jennifer passed hers they were talking away about the local football team. So that bit didn't bother her. She decided to apply.

Then something happened to change everything; she had to flee. An old flame of hers had come back into her life and turned up at her house very late one night. She wasn't there at the time and a new lodger, a young girl called Patricia, had just moved in. The story she told was terrifying. She had been alone in the house, dropping off to sleep when a lot of drunks, extremely noisy, started coming down the road. She expected them to go straight past, but to her horror they didn't. They started coming up the path. She hardly dared move. They started banging on the door, calling Jennifer's name and demanding she should come to the door. Patricia stayed very still with the blankets over her head. She thought that if the house remained in silence they would go away. There was no phone.

Then there was even more horror - they started breaking in. She had to get up. She called from the top of the stairs, 'What do you want?'

She heard one of them say, 'Oh there's a silly bitch in there'.

She didn't time how long they stayed for and found out next day that they had moved on when neighbours started showing an interest, shortly after one of them had thrown a milk bottle at the window and she heard a voice say, 'Don't do that Brian.'

Brian was the first man she'd taught to drive. He'd been lucky, as she did it for nothing. They had met at a night club and they had a bit of a fling. He seemed all right, but he was very frightened of his mother. She'd had one baby after another and put them into homes.

As a child he'd been fostered out all over the place. He was also unemployed. It would be a big help if he could drive a car.

The first time they went out it was the middle of the night, so they had the road to themselves. It was only the second time he had sat behind a wheel - the first had been with his brother. His steering was atrocious, and he was all over the place. In fact, his brother had been terrified and would never go out with him again. But Jennifer carefully taught him to steer, although it took them several hours. They had to keep having breaks, and they were twice stopped by the police.

After this she went out with him regularly and he made steady progress. It wasn't two steps forward and one step back, as with many. That was except one time when they had been on quite a long journey, they'd had a day out in Wales, and he had driven there and back. He did very well, but next day he was flat out and was stalling the engine on the least little hill. She had to assure him that he just needed a rest, he hadn't gone back to lesson one. It interested them both how a lorry driver can drive all day, and then get up next morning and do it all over again. It took her back to her childhood when she was learning to read. She had such a long book to get through. It was so interesting. She was dying to know the end of the story and she was managing it so well. The suddenly she collapsed and someone else had to read the end to her.

Brian passed his test second time, four and a half months after she first went out with him. They then went their separate ways, or so she thought, until he made this vicious attack on her.

The girl Patricia who had been so frightened was a do-gooder, and saw herself as a very compassionate person. She had a sly way of being nasty. She had no thought whatsoever for Jennifer. One would expect her not to be pleasant after an experience like that, but she was doing things which were not excusable in the name of caring. For example, she started saying, 'You are to warn people this house is dangerous.', knowing full well that remarks like that were very upsetting to someone who was so sorry and embarrassed about it all and who also felt quite traumatized. Patricia had other ways of having a sly dig and seemed very much to resent Jennifer. She later did a lot more in the name of caring, but her heart was of stone.

But at that time Jennifer was only suspicious, and Patricia's boyfriend moved in with their dog. They said they now felt safe, but Jennifer moved out and went to Madame Paree's. She didn't feel safe at all.

She felt sick. Why did Brian hate her? She'd done so much for him and now that he could drive he had got a job. She wondered what she was going to do about her career. She was now working the notice she'd been given, now that there had been one too many blow-ups about Miss Smith's Ladies Only Driving School and she was retiring. Miss Smith had decided to take early retirement and close down. Jennifer started her training as an examiner. 'Don't come back beating one another up,' the tutor would say to them as they went out in twos to examine one another. They'd laugh, yet some of them would come back almost fighting. She passed her test second time and started a job straight away. She was now thirty.

Her first day was very bad and she only passed two people; the rest were nowhere near test standard. The second day wasn't good either, until on the last test Mrs Jones came along. She was 64, had grey hair, looked frail and was extremely nervous. But weren't they all? Jennifer, fed up with everything, knew she should be smiling more but soon decided not to bother. As the test continued smoothly she realised that Mrs Jones was very passable. She remained sitting sullenly next to her, for she was sure it wouldn't be long before she'd get the poor, wretched woman grinning all over her face. Mrs Jones passed first time.

The third day things went splendidly and she passed nearly all of the candidates. On her fourth day, some of them were so bad that she had to physically intervene with the driving of the car. When she arrived home at Madame Paree's, she lay on her back flat out on the bed. The radio was on and they were talking about the driving test. Someone was saying that some of the test should be taken on the motorway. She screamed out, 'On the motorway? Where are they going to get the examiners from?'

Next day a candidate told her that someone who hadn't passed their test had caused so much trouble that they had had to call the police. This candidate wondered what all the commotion was about. It hadn't stopped him driving as he didn't mind taking a car out on the road without a licence.

Why had he bothered to take a test, and why was there all this commotion when he didn't pass? It didn't stop him driving. She said to Jennifer, 'It seems to be the worst thing you can do, to criticise someone's driving.' Someone had said that a Mr Sampson had taken his driving test four times, but in fact he had passed third time. He was talking about it as though he wanted to go round to the house of the woman who had been told this to put her straight. People were saying it wasn't like him. They said he was a professor at the university and should be above such things. Of course he wouldn't have done that, yet it was noticed. It's the worst thing you can do, to criticize someone's driving.

As time went by Jennifer felt very alone in her room on her own. She started going out a little and meeting people. Yet so much revolved around drinking and pubs, and she didn't want to be always doing that. At weekends she went to a night club with some girls she'd met, but she never drove. She depended on them for a lift. She'd pay them heavily for petrol and hope they'd oblige.

She didn't tell them what she did; she said she was a shorthand typist. If they knew the truth she'd have to walk. She'd already had some experience of people being afraid of accompanying an instructor. If she was a passenger in a car the driver would start to tell her everything he was doing, as though she should have some say in it. Yet she was certain that the worst drivers were the back seat drivers and the best drivers were the ones who could ignore them. She herself was a very bad driver; she would go along the road screaming at her passengers, 'It's ME that's driving this car, not you!' When she wasn't at work she wouldn't be watching how other people drove.

When she was coming back from night clubs she would crash down in the back seat. One night they were stopped by the police and the driver was breathalysed. Jennifer had had quite a bit to drink and was quite nervous, although none of them had done anything wrong. They got all three of them out and she was scared of being recognized. They were looking for something; maybe they thought there were drugs. They found nothing and the driver passed the breathalyser perfectly, so they let them go and Jennifer curled back up into a ball and went right back off to sleep.

Another time when she was sitting in the back seat she noticed a conversation between the two girls in the front. 'Why is it that women all think that thing between a man's legs is the ugliest thing that God ever created, yet men all think they've got the world's biggest prize?' said one girl. It was something she had wondered herself. And in her experience it was all men who thought that, including some very nice ones she'd known. She made some enquiries and discovered a theory amongst psychiatrists: women are supposed to feel cut off, and wish they had one.

'How typical of men to come to that conclusion,' she thought, for at that time nearly all psychiatrists were men. When she told the girls this, they said, 'Doesn't that prove our point, how typical of men? Let's get a few women psychiatrists on the job.'

She heard about something which was a real eye opener. A woman who she taught to drive, a friend of her sister's called Ellen, was saying that she had learned in twelve lessons, yet Jennifer knew it was more like 112. When she first went out with Jennifer she had had no tuition as an instructor and had only vaguely considered being one. Ellen had never sat behind the wheel of a car before. When she first started to put her foot on the accelerator and take the other off the clutch she started to gasp in fear, 'It's moving! It's moving!' This was followed by practice in stopping and starting, and mad steering. She was all over the pavement on the wrong side of the road, missing everything by quarter of an inch. Other people said she had to go to a driving school and should be in a car with dual controls. But after a few lessons she changed completely; she could now steer. It was as though she'd seen a psychiatrist rather than a driving instructor.

Yet she was still a long, long way off being up to test standard and she had lesson after lesson, frequently going out between with Jennifer. If she had taken her test after twelve lessons it she would not have finished it. It would have been a walk back.

It was one calamity after another. Jennifer remembered being with her once when she knocked a road sign down - it broke into little pieces. They got out and started picking them up, but then they decided they'd better leg it, if you can call it that in a car. As they went they noticed a bus queue of people watching them. After that every time Jennifer's front bell went, she was afraid to go in case it was a policeman standing there and someone had taken down their number.

Yet Ellen got much better, until her passengers assumed that she had a full licence. She would drive herself to work each morning through a busy town and then back again. She had her flatmate with her, who worked in a nearby office. She referred to this as 'going out very occasionally with someone in between lessons,' but in fact it was every morning and evening for a year, for nearly an hour a day.

People should not think there is something wrong with them if it's taking them a long time to learn to drive. Maybe there was something wrong with the person who said they had learnt so easily and quickly.

Jennifer could accept as lot of claims. One man told her he had had to take his driving test four times, but as he only had three lessons in between the first and the fourth he could say he had nearly passed first time. She also accepted it when a Mrs Ashley told her she had only taken it twice. She said 'I did something so very silly the second time I took it that I'm not going to call it a test.' Maybe she could say she failed on nerves the second time and she most certainly made no claims she had only had a few lessons or that she'd had no practice in between them. Jennifer reckoned she could say that she passed her driving test second time and an honesty test first time, but she wasn't having it that Ellen had passed on 12 lessons.

People didn't seem to realise why sometimes it wasn't the driving examiner who was such a nasty man but the instructor, because it would be his car that would be smashed up in the test and not the examiner's.

Jennifer decided that too much of her money was going on drink, even if it was mostly at weekends and she always had it under control. She would wake up every Sunday morning with a headache. One such morning she got up and wandered down the road and into a church. It was a long time since she'd taken communion. She sat at the back hoping her breath didn't still smell of alcohol. She picked up a book about forgiveness, and remembered another where the wife of a misogynist didn't agree with it. Jennifer had the subject on her mind. In that book the woman had been so bitter - her husband was in prison for sexually abusing their daughter - that they had even investigated whether he had raped her. Yet some of the congregation still wrote to him while he was there and said he was a sinner who should be forgiven. They said he would be welcomed back amongst the congregation when he came out. That was very hard on his wife and daughter, who also went to that church.

Jennifer thought about it. Maybe the woman had completely misinterpreted everything that was said. The church has to make it clear what it means by forgiving. That person should not be free to upset again, especially in a church. And surely when the church does so much counselling they would get professional advice. They must know something about misogyny, especially as it is taught to everyone everywhere. There something inside a church that can override the opinion of a psychologist. Jennifer wondered how the church could say that everyone was redeemable.

She started whispering about it to the woman sitting next to her, Sandra. She said, 'A man who truly repented would go to another church.' Sandra told her how she had once trembled with fear about it. Her sister, though not a Christian, and it was nothing whatsoever to do with the church, had been fanatical about not bearing grudges and not saying nasty things about people. You couldn't say for example, 'I'm making no appointments with him, he'll be late.'

The conversation got so interesting that even when the rest of the congregation stood up to sing, Jennifer and Sandra still sat there whispering. Whenever Sandra's sister came to the house Sandra would disappear upstairs. She was afraid to say anything in case her sister jumped down her throat and said she was bearing grudges. She would sometimes rehearse how to say something as though she was rehearsing her lines for a play, and then she would fail. Again she would be told it was a nasty thing to say about someone. It was making her quite neurotic.

It worried her. In a real crisis would her sister do something dangerous when forgiving someone, and put other people at risk? Then it was put to the test. The cousin had been to the house and been quite violent with her. After that neither she nor her mother would let him into the house. He showed no sign of any remorse, and there was every possibility he would do it again. Both she and her mother tried to explain this to the sister on the phone. She didn't agree. She said, 'It was quite some time ago.'

'But in this case it doesn't make it any less likely he won't do it again,' said Jennifer.

When Sandra came out of the phone box she was in a state of shock. Now she knew. Her sister would open the door and let anyone in, even if they were likely to be violent. She wondered if she would do that if it was she who was going to be beaten up and not Sandra.

She was shaking with fear. She went into a pub, sat quietly at a table with someone else having a quiet drink, then realised people were looking round at her. She was noticeably agitated, so she went round the block for a walk. Two days later she and her mother had a letter from the sister saying, 'I'm sorry my mother and sister have become grudge bearers.' She just didn't understand. The sad thing was Sandra never spoke to her again. She didn't dare.

After church they had cups of tea and biscuits in the church hall next door. Then they went outside and Jennifer stood on the pavement waving goodbye to her as she drove off with her husband. There were L plates on and clearly she was a learner. 'Oh please don't turn up at the centre tomorrow to take a test,' she thought. She would refuse to take her, saying she knew her. It would have been a shock for Sandra to see her there as Jennifer had told her a lie. She had said she was a shorthand typist.

After this Jennifer attended that church more often, and she would go to the church hall on a Saturday morning, when she could have a cooked breakfast. She met Sandra and her husband Sam quite a bit. She had always thought it was a mistake husband and wife teaching one another to drive a car, as so often it finishes up with them falling out. Sandra and Sam were no exception. In jokes, it's the man shouting at the woman because she's such a bad learner; in fact it was she who was shouting at him because he was such a bad teacher.

When they had first started going out together, Sandra thought that if anyone hooted at her, he would say, 'NOW look at what a fool you are making of yourself.' But no. It would make him absolutely furious. No one was to hoot at her. She didn't know she was so precious but it seemed she was; he wouldn't have it, no one was to criticize her. She would sometimes shout at him, and sometimes say to him gently 'Leave it, leave it will yer! I know, he hooted, he shouldn't, you're right and he's wrong, but leave it.'

Then one day Sam got out of the car and had it out with the man in the car behind him. When they got home she had it out with him. There was to be no brawling in the street. She was never so glad as when she passed her driving test. Now she could go out on her own and people could hoot at her as much as they liked.

Sam told Jennifer something that she would not be repeating to Sandra. She knew how wild it would make her. He said, 'When you teach your wife to drive, the first thing you teach her is how to reverse. Then if the man behind you hoots you get her to back into the front of him. Then you get out of your car and swear point blank, it was he who drove into the back of her.'

Jennifer decided to turn Patricia out of her house. She wasn't a pleasant character and she'd been suspicious of her right from the start. Her sly way of having digs at her about the attack on the house was only the beginning of it; in fact Jennifer did wonder if she was jealous of her because she hadn't got a house herself.

She also saw herself as a very compassionated person, yet clearly she wasn't. Jennifer wondered what that was all about. It started when she overheard someone saying to her, 'Are you sympathizing with people who owe money?' She was. The person who was asking her sounded disgusted. Jennifer's heart sank. It was a case of 'Look at how caring I am'. And she was doing more than that. She worked in a library and was being very reluctant to help victims with getting information. It was a typically sly way of hers of being nasty in the name of caring, though she thought it was admirable. When challenged about it she went on and on; no one else could get a word in, and she finished up by saying, 'A lot of them will, I won't, I'm soft.' Yet she was hard, very hard.

Is there any connection between seeing yourself as a compassionate person and indulging in eating? Although some grossly overweight people are some of the loveliest people you could ever imagine meeting, this was the second time Jennifer had been nauseated by someone's talk on 'caring'. Obviously it was hypocritical, and both times they were very fat.

Something else struck her as strange. According to Patricia it was poor people who were generous with money, while the rich were all very mean. When Jennifer had sometimes collected money for charity she found it quite noticeable that she got more in middle-class areas. She realised that it might be the poor who gave more in relative terms, but not in actual money. But Patricia wasn't having any of it. She wouldn't even accept that.

She also claimed great poverty herself. She seemed to think there was something picturesque in looking sweet and poor. Yet clearly she had money tucked away somewhere, as at times she would have quite a bit to spend.

Yet it was none of this that put Jennifer off. She heard that Patricia had stayed for a while in a very old lady's house, pleading poverty and scrounging. She didn't have any rent to pay, she went there as a friend, but if she was in a position to help she always refused. The old lady had a paper round to do each week and she didn't want to lose it. It would have been a big help if Patricia had been willing to come out with her sometimes, but she had one excuse after another not to.

Then the daughter came to stay. She helped a lot with the paper round but one night she had to finish early to go babysitting, so she left her mother with Patricia to finish it off. Before she went she asked her mother if she could go to the take away for her to get something for her to eat. She waited and waited and then decided she wasn't coming. Who could blame her in weather like this? She'd decided to go straight home. It didn't matter, the television was good, the children were in bed, and the daughter could help herself to tea and biscuits.

Then at ten o'clock she saw her. Amongst all the snow that was falling, in the dusk, her mother was walking up the path carrying her supper for her. Patricia had left her a long time ago. She justified leaving the old lady like this by saying her wages were so little it was encouraging capitalism to help give out the newspapers. She was helping the poor to refuse. The daughter said, 'Out!'

That had been some time ago, but now Jennifer was saying 'Out' Olive went to live there instead. She had considered asking Clare if she would like to go but found that the battered man hadn't spent quite all the time in the attic. He and Clare had had a few chats together and had come to some agreement. He could stay in her house, which had been empty for some time. It would be somewhere his kids could come and see him. Clare, not even having a fling with him, had decided to convert the downstairs into a bed sitter, and though they would be living separately there would be someone in the house with her.

It amused Jennifer that another battered man took his place. They passed each other in the hall; one was going out as the other was going in. He'd been so desperate he had paid a month's rent in advance. She thought about the men she worked with, the driving examiner who said it was women who had taught him a few new words, and still looking amused she told Madame Paree, 'Sounds like it's good for business, I'll get a few more battered men in for you if you like.'

So Olive moved into Jennifer's house. She had just had another shock; she had heard from Sarah, the girl who had first looked after little Nigel, the one whose father was suspected of murdering a prostitute, and more evidence had appeared that he had indeed done it. However there was nothing they could do about it as he had been dead for two years. She also knew what had happened before in Jennifer's house, how it had been attacked by Brian and some youths, but that was very small compared with all that Sarah was telling and in any case it was quite some time ago and she was certain it wouldn't happen again.

Then shortly after she'd moved in she was woken up in the early hours of the morning in the same way Patricia had been. There was a banging on the front door and men aggressively demanding to speak to Jennifer. She ran out of the back door, into the back yard next door and banged furiously at their door, but no one was in. Throughout it all she could hear all the rowdy noise of these yobbos. She could hear obscenities being shouted, 'Jennifer, Jennifer, open up this door!' and things being thrown at the window. In fact it was so loud they had not heard her furious banging on the back door next door.

She ran down the alleyway in her bare feet and came face to face with a wall, wondering if she could jump over. Then she did a very sharp U turn and started to run back. How could she get out? She could find no house to go to; all the walls were high and all the gates were locked. Then she found a little alleyway she could escape down. As she ran past Jennifer's she noticed a light going on and thought they had broken in. Then she came to the end of the alley; she was now in a street. She was free.

But what was she going to do? She wore only her dressing gown and had no money, no coat, no shoes. She went on in a state of shock, glad to be alive, not thinking about where she was going or how late it was getting.

Suddenly she was in the town centre. She heard a man's voice, a voice she had heard before, a voice that was gentle and nice, and it was someone who seemed to know her.

It was the young man in the bookshop. She'd been in there quite a few times. It had been embarrassing to ask a man for books on men who hate women, yet he'd been so helpful, finding books for her and ordering them.

'Whatever is it?' he asked her. She nearly burst into tears as she told him everything about that night.

'Come in' he told her, 'Come inside.'

She could hardly believe her luck. Before she crashed out on the couch she made a 999 phone call to say that people were breaking into Jennifer's. He then put a blanket on her and she lay there motionless, in a state of shock.

She looked around the room, at the furniture, and felt she had been there before; it made her curious, for she felt she had sat on this couch before too. Then suddenly she saw something which made her sit upright. It was a photograph of a little boy; Nigel, the boy she had neglected. She looked at the young man from the bookshop, about to ask him, 'Who's that?', but she had no need to. She could see the face in the picture. It was Nigel.

He had recognized her from the first time she had gone into the shop. An adult doesn't change much, but a child does. 'Oh Nigel, can you forgive me?' she said. He looked amused and said, 'Stop being so daft.'

Then they heard someone coming in through the back door downstairs, and then as large as life she saw him on the stairs; his father. She recognized him at once. 'It was my mother who was the bitch, a wicked bitch,' said Nigel. 'But not you, and at least I had my father.'

'Well a man's place is in the home, and your father was always in the home.'

The three of them laughed together.

She woke up next morning very early, at five o'clock. He had found some clothes for her to put on and she began to creep out. She felt as if she was intruding, but she certainly intended coming back to thank them both. Then she saw a light go on. He was getting up. Nigel quickly appeared and told her to stay. 'I feel like an intruder' she told him. How could she accept such kindness from someone who she felt she hadn't been kind to at all, when he was little and needed her?

'You're not intruding, we want you here,' he told her.

They sat down and talked. He explained that when his father had left his mother, she hadn't minded him taking Nigel with him. He had then had a very good nanny who had stayed some years, and he never went to the boarding school they put him down for. After he left school at sixteen he and his father opened up the bookshop together. It was a perfect job for him, no exams to pass. Nigel was no good at passing exams.

'But I have to go home to my husband sometimes' she told him.

She went, but never for long. She had a room in the flat above the bookshop she could always go back to, there was always something useful that could be found in the shop for her to do, and she did hope eventually to be able to get a living-in job looking after some child.

Her husband was happy too. He had found Jeanette. They were partners in hate, and she was a woman who thrived on excitement. Neither of them thought anything of getting up in the middle of the night to have a row. Yet he still wanted to be married to Olive.